Drum Backbeats
ENCYCLOPEDIA
HUNDREDS OF USEFUL BACKBEATS FOR THE DRUMSET

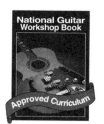

JOHN THOMAKOS

Alfred, the leader in educational publishing, and the National Guitar Workshop, one of America's finest guitar schools, have joined forces to bring you the best, most progressive educational tools possible. We hope you will enjoy this book and encourage you to look for other fine products from Alfred and the National Guitar Workshop.

D1501311

This book was acquired, edited and produced by Workshop Arts, Inc., the publishing arm of the National Guitar Workshop.
Nathaniel Gunod, acquisitions, editor
Michael Rodman, editor
Gary Tomassetti, music typesetter
Timothy Phelps, interior design
CD Recorded and engineered by Scott Smith at Oak-Lea Manor, Maryland
Cover photo courtesy of Yamaha Corporation of America

ISBN 0-7390-2344-6 (Book)
ISBN 0-7390-2345-4 (Book & CD)

Contents

About the Author

John Thomakos was born in Baltimore, Maryland and began playing drums at the age of four. He graduated from the Baltimore School for the Arts as a percussion/music major with a scholarship award to the Berklee College of Music in Boston, Massachusetts. He also holds a Certificate with Honors and an award for Best Funk Drummer from the Musicians Institute, Percussion Institute of Technology in Los Angeles, California.

John has since continued a successful professional career as a freelance drummer, author, and teacher. His educational material has been featured in *Modern Drummer* magazine. He maintains a busy schedule of teaching and performances in the United States, England and Canada. His playing can be heard on radio ads for BMW, on the television shows *Brooklyn South*, *Jack and Jill* and *That's Life*, and in the movies *The Smokers*, *About Sarah* and *The Girl Next Door*.

Acknowledgments

My sincere appreciation goes out to the follow people: Gary Rosensweig, Shea Welsh, Scott Smith, Jennifer Smith, Carl Filipiak, George Mexis, Glen Workman, Jim Jones, Wes Crawford, Ron Kraus, Hope Gerecht, Mike Davis, Meg Murray and Rob Rent. Thanks to Nat Gunod, Gary Tomassetti and Tim Phelps at the National Guitar Workshop for bringing this publication to fruition. Special thanks also to my many teachers, mentors and colleagues. Very special thanks to my father, George Thomakos, Valerie Smith and Stella Thomakos. Thanks to Scott Smith for his work on the CD for this book, and to Julie Baker and Jon Grose for proofreading the original manuscript.

This book is dedicated to my mother, Maria Thomakos.

Introduction

Backbeat grooves, grooves that have snare-drum accents on beats 2 and 4, are frequently the rhythmic foundation in blues, rock, pop, funk, gospel, soul, country, Latin and Caribbean music, as well as a variety of other styles. Because this form of rhythmic accompaniment crosses so many stylistic boundaries, it is important that every player realizes the full potential of backbeat grooves and practices them thoroughly—along with their practical and essential variations and embellishments. This requires the development of coordination, confidence and technical freedom. This book will help you with develop in these areas.

The goal of this book is to encourage and promote groove development and *pocket playing* (playing with a solid feel in good time) in backbeat grooves. The four main areas of concentration in this book are:

> Right-Hand Ostinatos—Section One
> Open Hi-Hat Development—Section Two
> Hi-Hat with the Foot—Section Three
> Snare-Drum Grace Notes—Section Four

Enjoy!

Time and Feel

Drummers are rarely hired solely on the basis of their "chops" (technique, fills, flashiness). The drummers that work the most—those who are in demand—are those who play with steady, solid time and a good feel. These drummers are what people often refer to as *pocket players*. Bandleaders and band members treasure them.

The main objective of a pocket player is to provide a solid rhythmic foundation for each song. Once this foundation has been established, fills and embellishments are used to support the song without jeopardizing the groove. The point here is to encourage groove and feel development first. Fills and flashiness are useless without a solid foundation.

The only way to understand the sensation of playing with solid time is to listen to and experience music that is played that way. You are what you listen to. See the Recommended Listening section on page 6.

Attitude and Execution

Many drum grooves are interchangeable from style to style—a country song and a heavy metal song, for example, may have the same basic drum groove. The key element that makes these grooves appropriate for a specific style is the *attitude* with which they are played. The attitude and emotion of the playing effectively alters the sound and feel which one produces on the instrument.

There are many other variables that distinguish one style from another. The drum set itself is often set up and/or altered by: tuning; head combinations; cymbal types and thicknesses; drumsticks of particular weight and design; brushes or other playing implements; playing techniques and varied recording techniques; the list goes on. But, before any of these sound-manipulating devices or techniques are implemented, the heart of the music—the emotion and attitude that the music is played with—is the uncompromising foundation of any song or style of music.

Learning by listening, developing the techniques to play what the music calls for and playing with other musicians are three essential areas of development. This book is designed to guide progress in these areas. The key is to enjoy the process.

Notation Legend

Here is a key to the drum set notation used in this book:

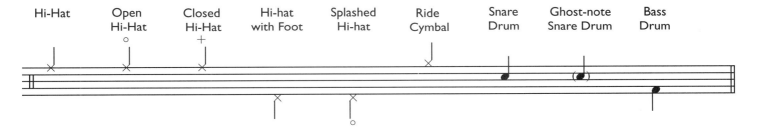

Hi-Hat | Open Hi-Hat | Closed Hi-Hat | Hi-hat with Foot | Splashed Hi-hat | Ride Cymbal | Snare Drum | Ghost-note Snare Drum | Bass Drum

The CD

A compact disc is available for this book. Using this disc will help make learning more enjoyable and the information more meaningful. Listening to it will help you play the correct rhythm and feel for each example. Every example performed on the CD is marked with this symbol:

Track 1

The track numbers below the symbol correspond to the example(s) you want to hear. For Section One, all 22 kick/snare grooves have been recorded without the hi-hat, and all 28 hi-hat grooves (one for each Part) have been recorded without the kick/snare grooves. Also, each of the 28 hi-hat grooves have been recorded with the first of the 22 kick/snare grooves. The rest of the examples in the book have been recorded in one track per page. Enjoy.

Recommended Listening

There is an overwhelming amount of recorded material that we can listen to for information, inspiration and enjoyment. In an effort to guide productive musical development through listening, below is a short list of essential "must have" recordings. These illustrate many of the ideas featured in this book.

Purchase one recording at a time. Take your time when listening. Spend weeks, if not longer, listening to and immersing yourself in just one recording. You will find that this concentrated listening approach will positively influence your playing.

James Brown—"Funk Power," "20 All-Time Greatest Hits" and "Motherlode"

Funkadelic—"Music for Your Mother"

Led Zeppelin— "Led Zeppelin" (box set) and "Boxed Set 2"

The Meters—"Funkify Your Life" (box set)

Sly & The Family Stone—"Anthology"

Stevie Wonder—"At the Close of the Century" (box set)

Tower of Power—"What Is Hip?"

Remember, YOU ARE WHAT you listen to.

Muscle Memory

Programming Perfection into Your Performance

Practice, practice, practice. If your goal is to develop your musical skills and be proficient at your instrument, you must practice regularly. Knowing exactly what to do when you practice is particularly important. To most people, the game plan seems obvious: Just try to figure out how to play whatever it is that you are working on and then make it sound better. That is definitely the right idea, but with some insight and knowledge about how we learn, you can begin to make your practice more productive and enjoyable and get successful results in less time.

First, let's define "practice." According to a respected dictionary, practice means: *To perform or work at something, so as to become proficient; to train by repeating exercises.* You may be wondering if the clichéd adage, "practice makes perfect" is really true. It all depends on how we go about doing it. A more accurate statement might be: "Perfect practice makes perfect."

Perfect practice (practice with few or no mistakes) makes perfect because our minds and bodies memorize movement through repetition. This is often called "muscle memory." Muscle memory is actually a mental function. The brain, which controls the body, learns the movements. Training the mind to make movements occur as if they were "automatic" is the key to performing any physical skill with consistency, confidence, ease and fluency. When we appreciate exactly how muscle memory programming takes place, we can begin to more effectively implement this idea in our learning and development.

"Muscle Memory" in Everyday Life and the Importance of Correct Repetition

Walking, running, riding a bike, writing, typing, tying a shoe, buttoning a shirt and thousands of other physical activities, which we easily perform daily, have been perfected through correct repetition. It is the same learning process coaches and athletes have used in training for years: programming and perfecting a golf swing, a gymnastics routine, a figure skating movement or a high dive. It is through correct repetition that we have trained our minds to make the muscles of our body perform these and other once-challenging tasks with ease.

Take a moment to observe your hands and fingers as you perform the simple task of tying a shoe. Do it slowly and watch each step carefully. This complicated procedure, which most of us struggled with at first, has now become perfected to the point of being a mindless task. As musicians, the goal is to achieve this level of comfort and confidence when playing our instruments.

Notice that observing the details of how to tie a shoe makes doing it more difficult. It's easier when we let muscle memory take over. When we are "programming" the movements, we have to perform this way—carefully observing every aspect of the movement to make sure it is perfect. But at some point, we have to break loose from controlling things and let the movements become automatic. This way, the mind can be taught to make the body perform amazing feats. Psychologists have labeled this state of seemingly effortless execution as *automaticity*. A more commonly used term describing the same phenomenon is "automatic pilot."

Imagine trying to teach someone that 2 + 2 = 4 but occasionally telling him or her that 2 + 2 = 5. This would be confusing. A similar confusion in learning takes place when practice is done too quickly with little or no control and frequent mistakes. This keeps us from making progress. The reason for this is that our mind memorizes movement in much the same way that it retains other information: through repetition and reinforcement. In other words, our mind/body is able to memorize and perfect consistently repeated movements. When we practice an exercise slowly, correctly and repeatedly, we are programming ourselves to correctly perform this movement on command. This is muscle memory.

Developing musical automaticity or muscle memory enables you to perform with total confidence, because your playing will require less mental effort. Your mind/body has been properly programmed and you can focus on other aspects of the performance—for example, dynamics, feel, singing while playing and musicality. Not even the adrenaline rush or anxiety of an important performance can interrupt the consistency and effectiveness of muscle memory.

Summary

The key to rapid learning and good playing is to slowly and correctly repeat whatever it is you are practicing with minimal mistakes. If you make too many mistakes—and repeat mistakes— you are not training yourself to play well; you are learning to make mistakes. Practicing is never neutral; you are either getting better or getting worse. Being mindful of the process of muscle memory programming can greatly accelerate your learning and make your practicing more productive, rewarding and fun.

"Not even the adrenaline rush or anxiety of an important performance can interrupt the consistency and effectiveness of muscle memory."

Three Steps to More Productive Practice

Listed below are general guidelines for employing muscle memory programming. If you're working on something new, start with Step One. If your goal is to polish and perfect something you can already play, skip to Step Three.

Step One: Break down whatever it is that you are working on into small sections. The length of these sections will vary depending on the example. Some passages may be easier to learn if shortened to one or two beats, others could be one or two measures. The objective is to avoid biting off more than you can chew. Learn small sections first, and then put them together.

Step Two: Practice playing through each small section very slowly. At first, play so slowly that it is nearly impossible to make a mistake. Mistakes are often likely at first, but are avoidable if you practice slowly enough. Develop one section at a time. Practice this way until you can easily and comfortably play the section through without mistakes. Once you have two sections prepared, join them together and practice them as one. Continue developing each section separately and piecing them together until you have reassembled the whole passage. This is the most challenging part, so be very patient.

Step Three: Once you can play the entire passage at a very slow tempo, keep it there! Repeat the example in four-minute blocks and take frequent short breaks. The more correct repetitions at a slow tempo, the better. The breaks will help you retain a high level of concentration and prevent you from making mistakes due to a lack of attention.

Use a digital timer to keep track of these four-minute practice blocks. This will allow you to completely focus on the exercise. When the timer sounds after four minutes, take a break. Relax and breathe for 30 seconds to a minute between each four-minute practice block. Repeat this cycle throughout your practice session. This is muscle memory programming at work.

The Big Picture

Although you make progress every time you practice correctly, some more difficult techniques and passages may take months or even years to perfect. Once you begin to enjoy the never-ending learning process, your progress enters upon a new path. Never be discouraged by obstacles or failure—both are a major parts of learning. With focused persistence, perseverance and patience, you will eventually attain all of your goals.

"I think everybody's got the ability to have good time. But if you don't focus on it … you won't play as well."

Clyde Stubblefield
Modern Drummer, 1999

Steve Gadd, *was born in Rochester, New York on April 9, 1945. Gadd is one of the greatest drummers of all time. Any recording which features Gadd on drums is a musical treat and a lesson. Check out his playing on the 1979 George Benson release "Livin' Inside Your Love" and on the timeless classic* 50 Ways To Leave Your Lover *on Paul Simon's "Still Crazy after All These Years."*

Steve Ferrone, *known for his rock solid time and great feel, spent most of the 1970s performing and recording with The Average White Band. Since then he has been one of the most in-demand drummers in the world.*

Section One

Right-Hand Ostinatos

This section features 28 different right-hand *ostinatos* (repeated accompaniment patterns) to be played on the hi-hat. For accelerated learning, the practice grooves in the bass and snare drums are the same in every part of the first section (Parts One–Twenty-Eight).

Many of the ostinatos in Section One vary by their accent pattern alone. This change appears minute on paper, but the change in sound and feel is dramatic. The objective is to be able to perform each ostinato while working through all of the grooves in each part. The main goal, however, is to eventually incorporate these ideas into any groove.

"I do tend to lead with my hi-hat. My weapons of choice are hi-hat, snare drum and bass drum. That's where I focus ... the hi-hat is important to me."

Steve Ferrone
Modern Drummer, May 1995

The Hi-Hat Grooves

Below is a list of the ostinatos that are featured in this section. It is recommended that the beginner and intermediate player begin with Part Four and Part Eight of this section (eighth notes and sixteenth notes). After they have been mastered, the rest of Section One will be easier to develop.

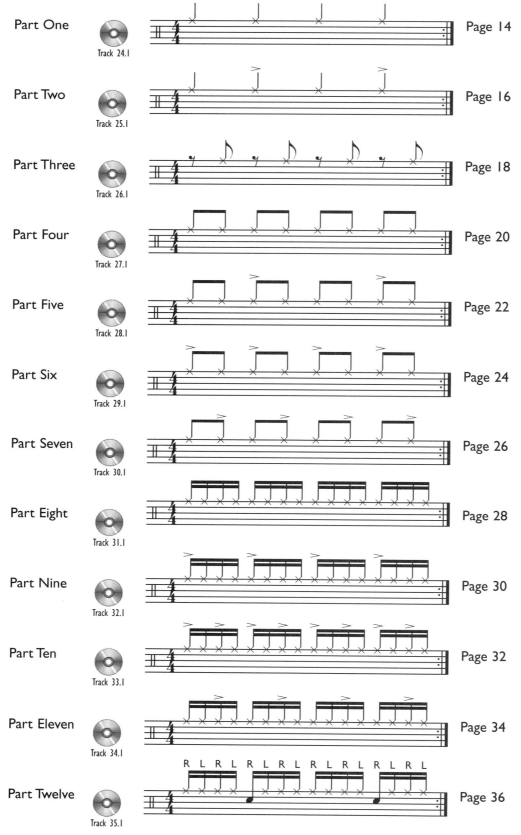

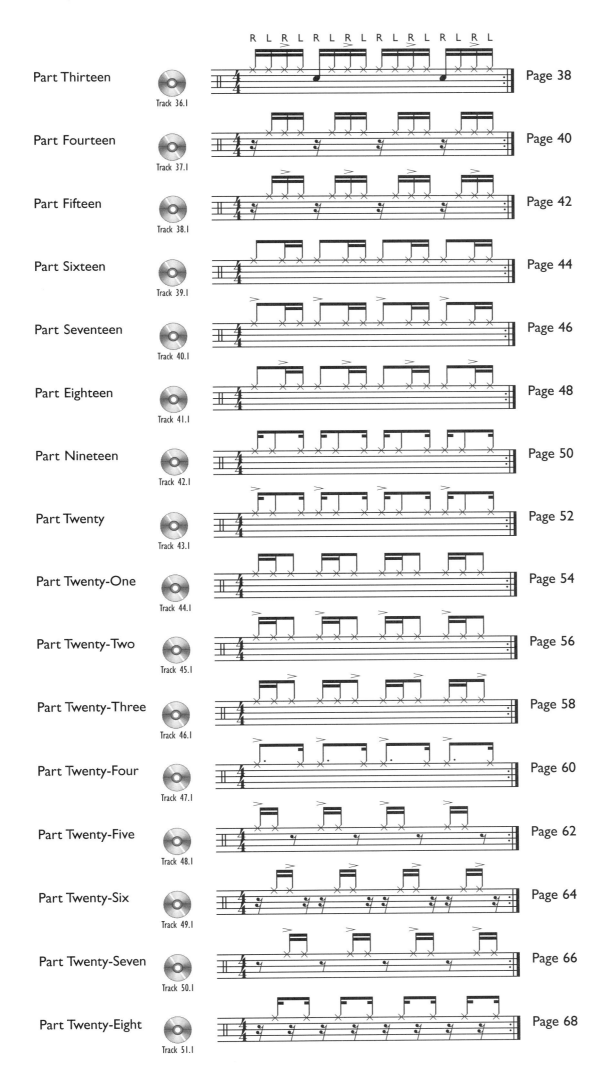

Part One—Quarters

Notice the use of *ghost notes* in examples 18 and 20 on page 15. Written in parentheses, ghost notes are subtle, unaccented snare-drum notes. They are played at about half the volume of normal snare-drum notes. See Section Five (starting on page 89) for more about ghost notes.

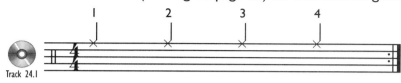

Track 24.1

When we count eighth notes, we count as follows: "1-&-2-&-3-&-4-&," and so on. The &s are the offbeats. When we count sixteenth notes, we count as follows: "1-e-&-ah, 2-e-&-ah, 3-e-&-ah, 4-e-&-ah."

(🎵) = Ghost Note

Part Two—Quarters with Accents on 2 and 4

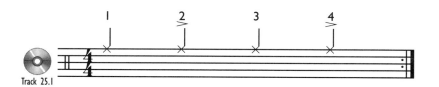

Track 25.1

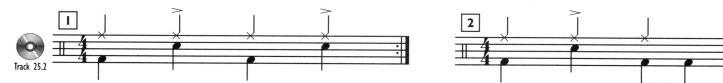

Track 25.2

1

2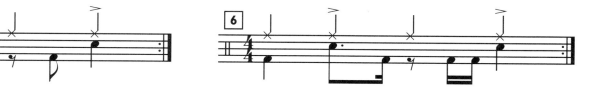

3

4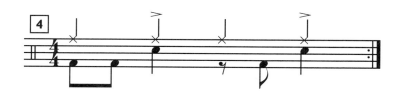

5

6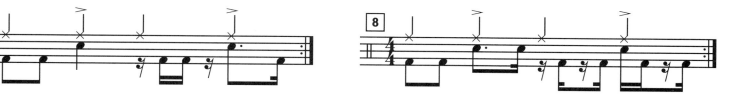

7

8

9

10

Part Three—Eighths on the Offbeats

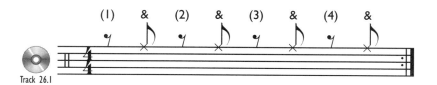

Track 26.1

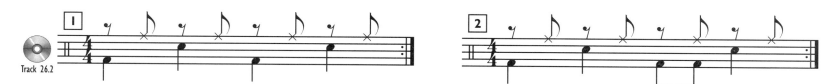

Track 26.2

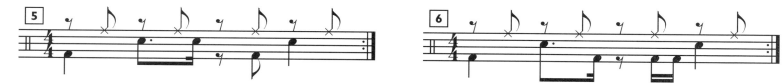 

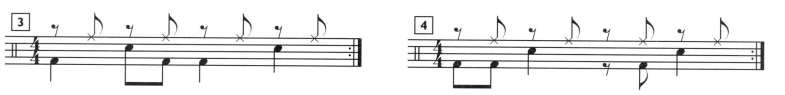

 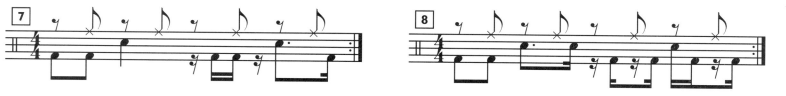

 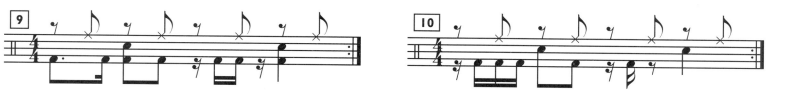

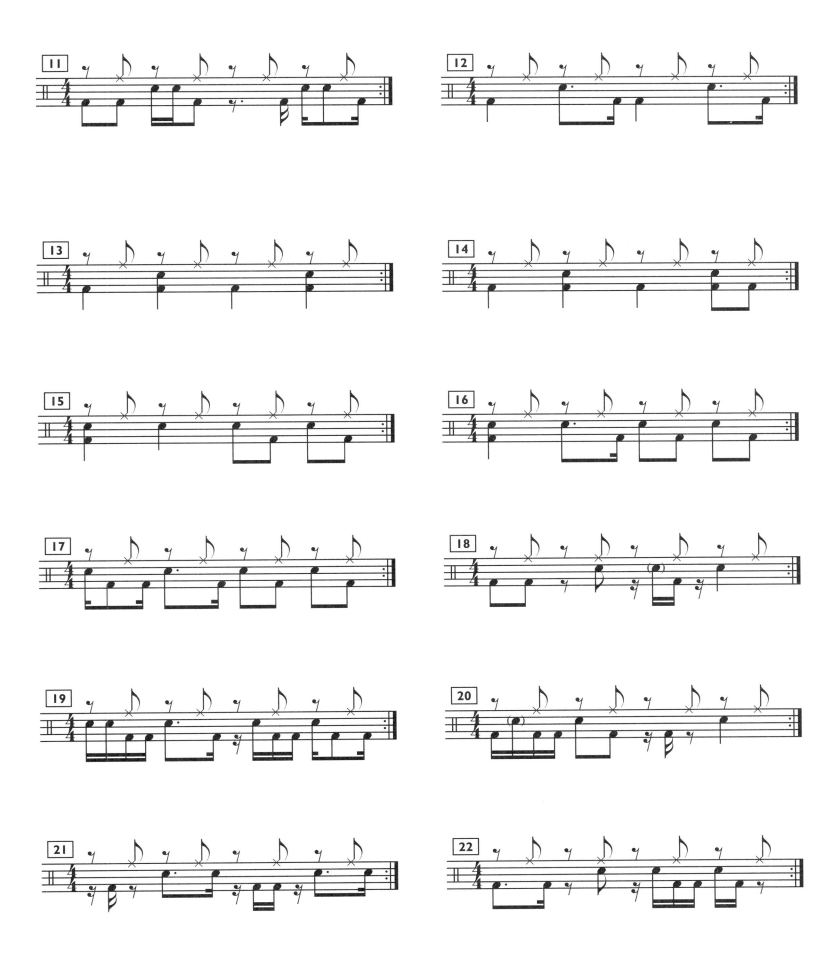

Part Four—Eighths

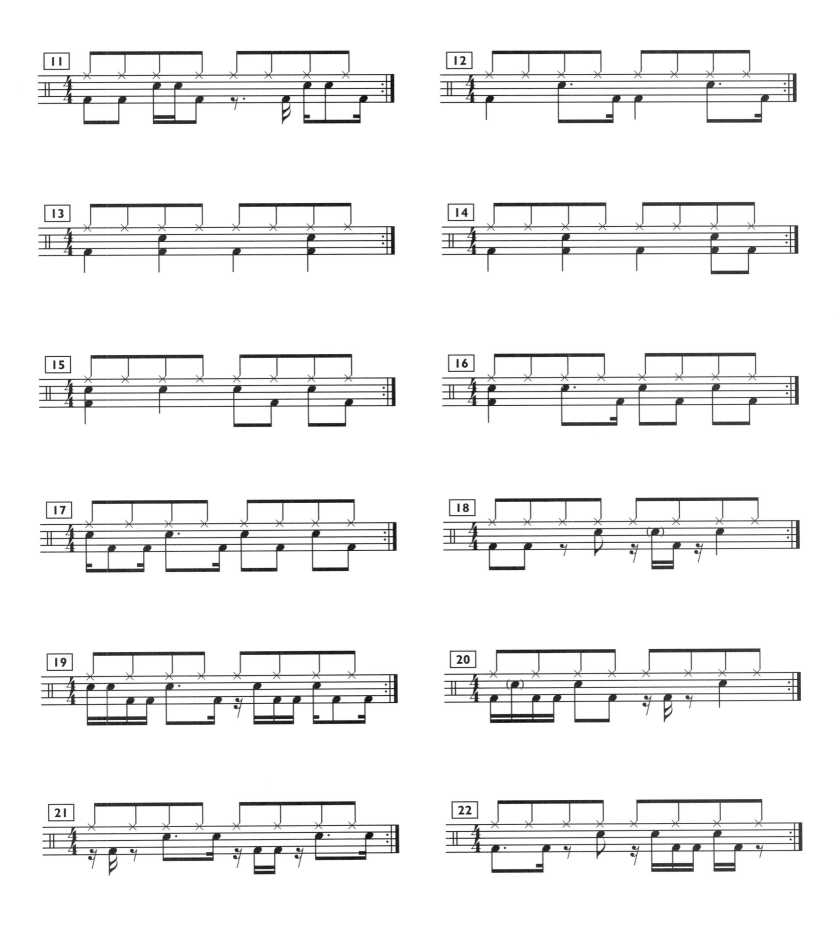

Part Five—Eighths with Accents on 2 and 4

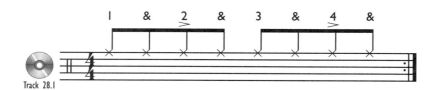

Track 28.1

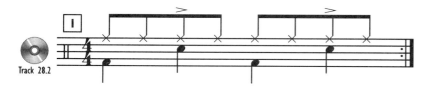

Track 28.2

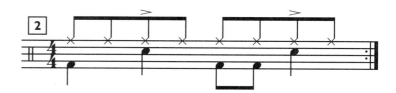

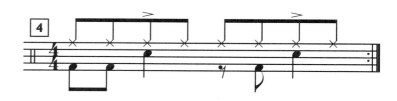

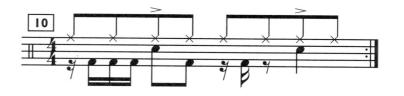

23

Part Six—Eighths with Accents on the Onbeats

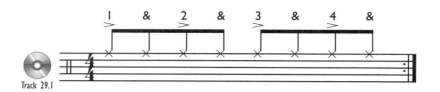

Track 29.1

Track 29.2

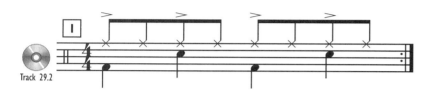

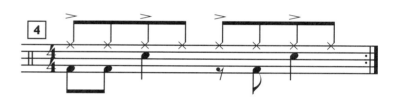

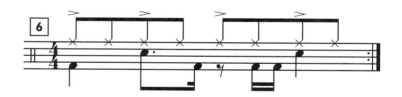

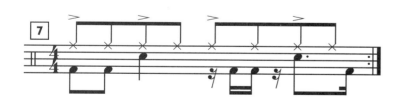

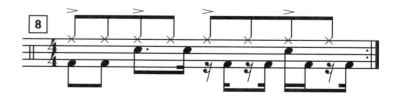

Part Seven—Eigths with Accents on the Offbeats

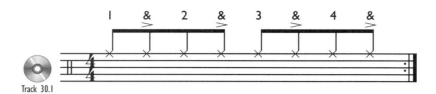

Track 30.1

Track 30.2

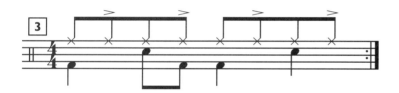

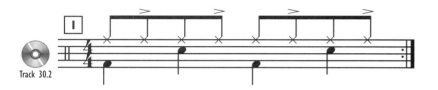

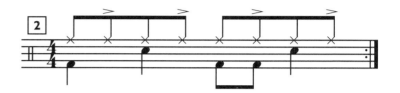

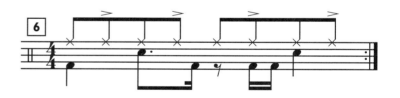

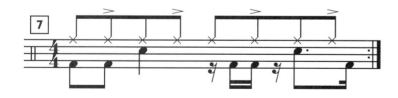

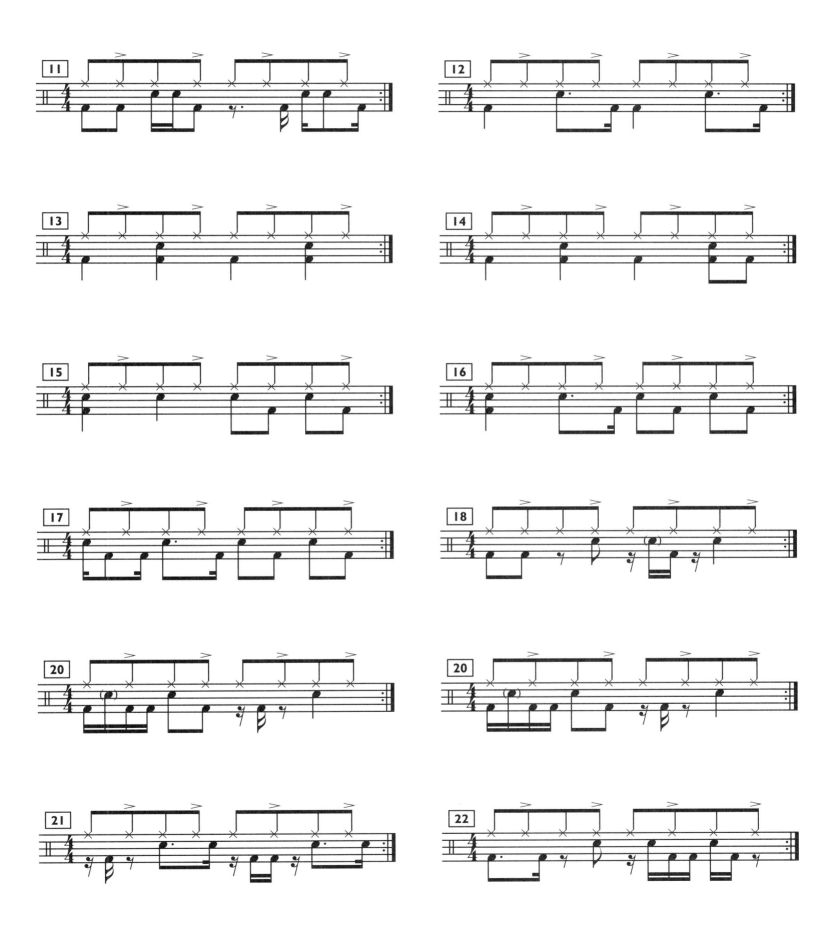

Part Eight—Sixteenths

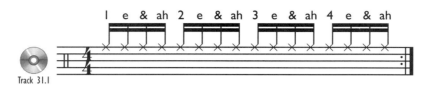

Track 31.1

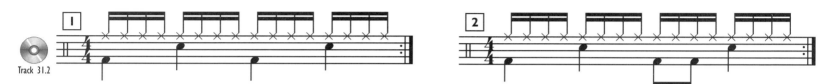

Track 31.2

1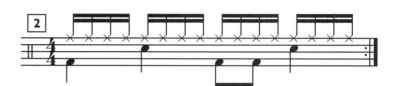

3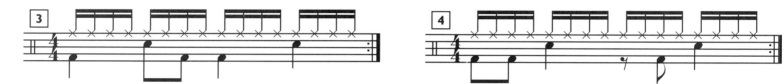

4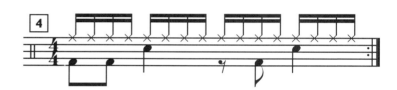

5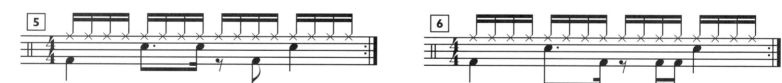

6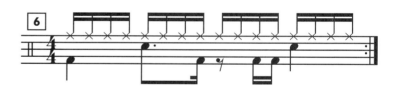

7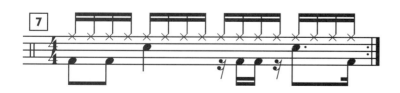

8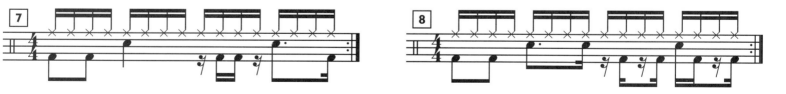

9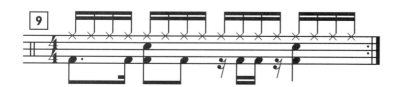

10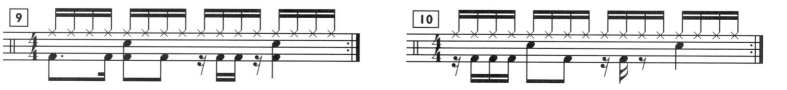

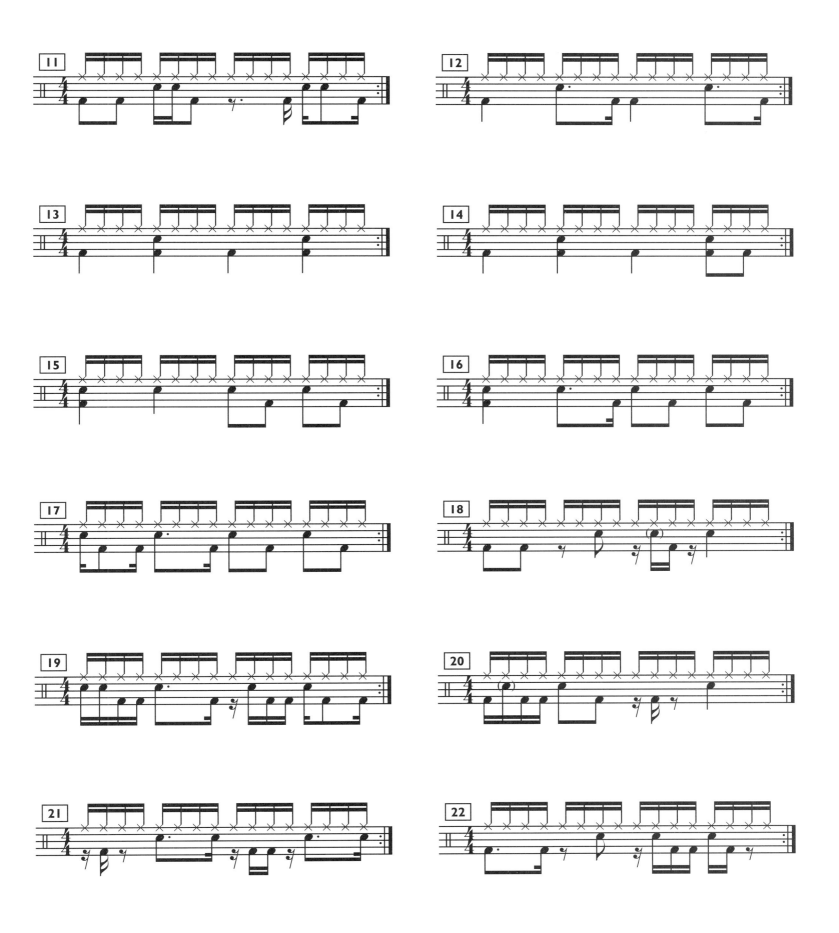

Part Nine—Sixteenths with Accents on the Onbeats

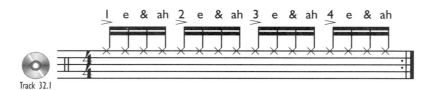

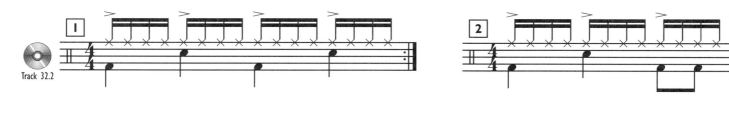
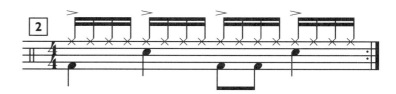

Track 32.1

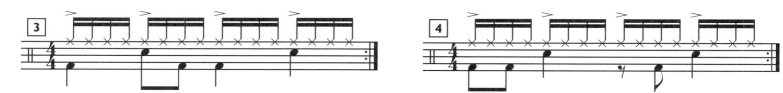
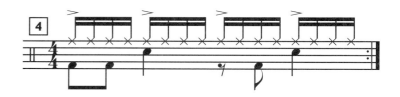

Track 32.2

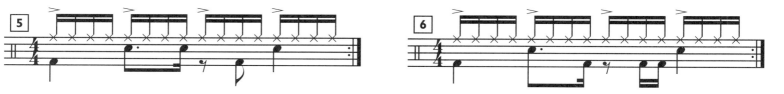
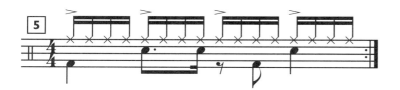

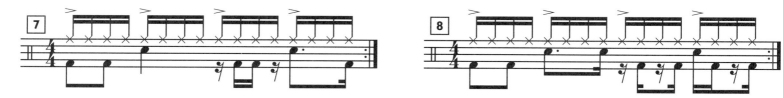
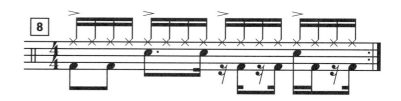

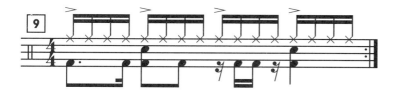
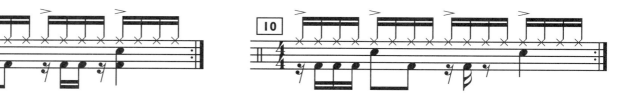

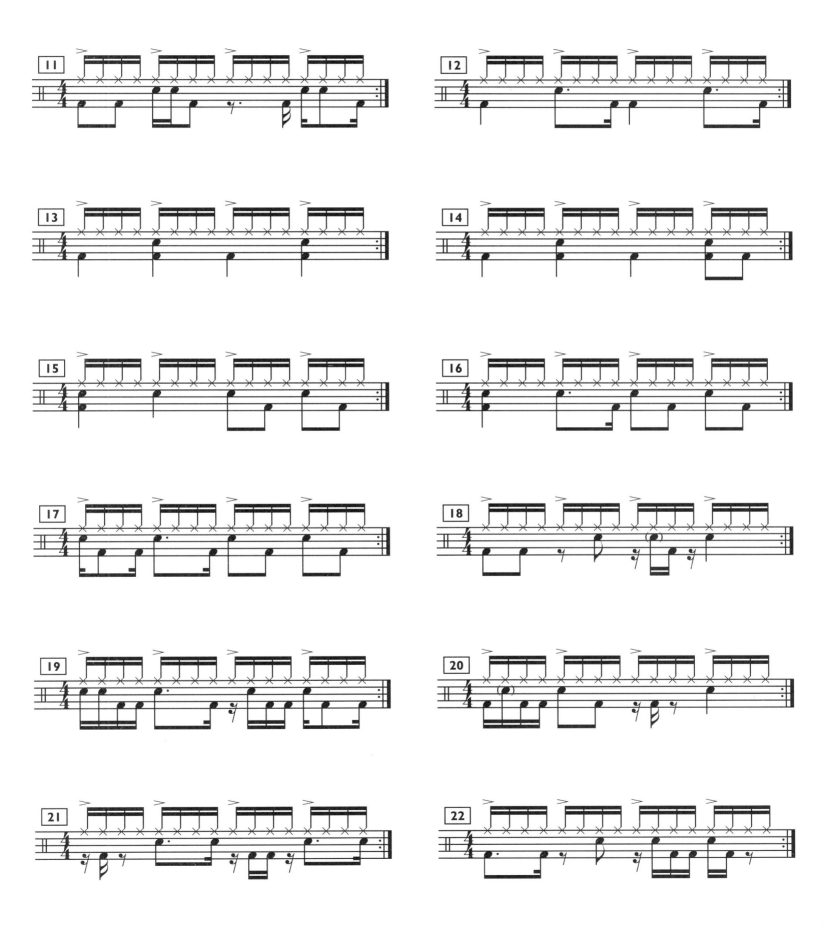

Part Ten—Sixteenths with Accents on the Eighths

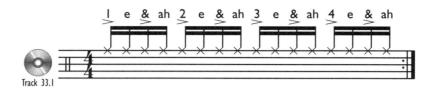

Track 33.1

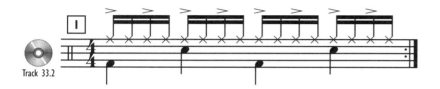

Track 33.2

1
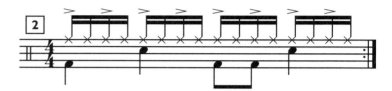
2

3
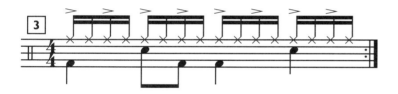
4

5
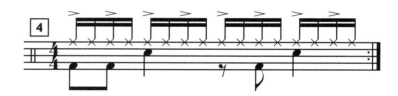
6

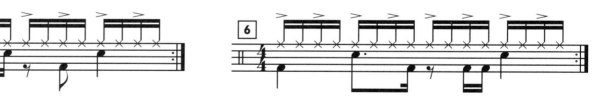

7

8

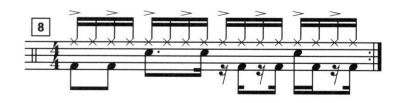

9
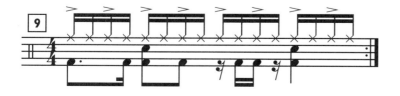
10

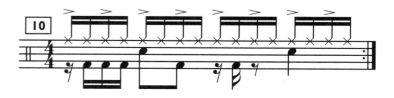

Part Eleven—Sixteenths with Accents on the Offbeats

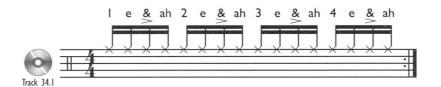

Track 34.1

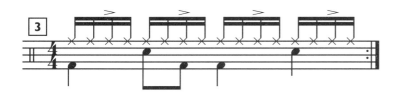 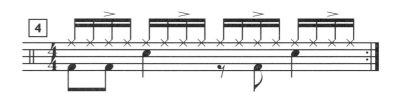

Track 34.2

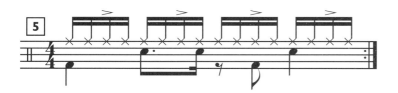 

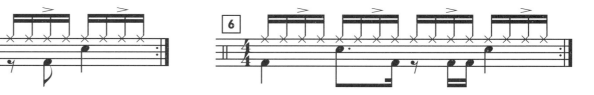

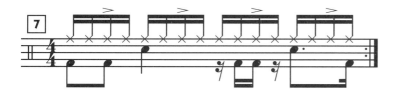 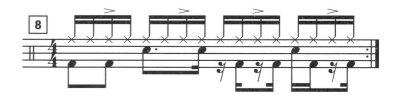

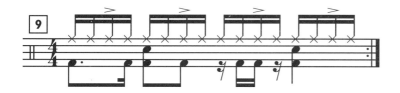 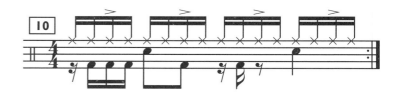

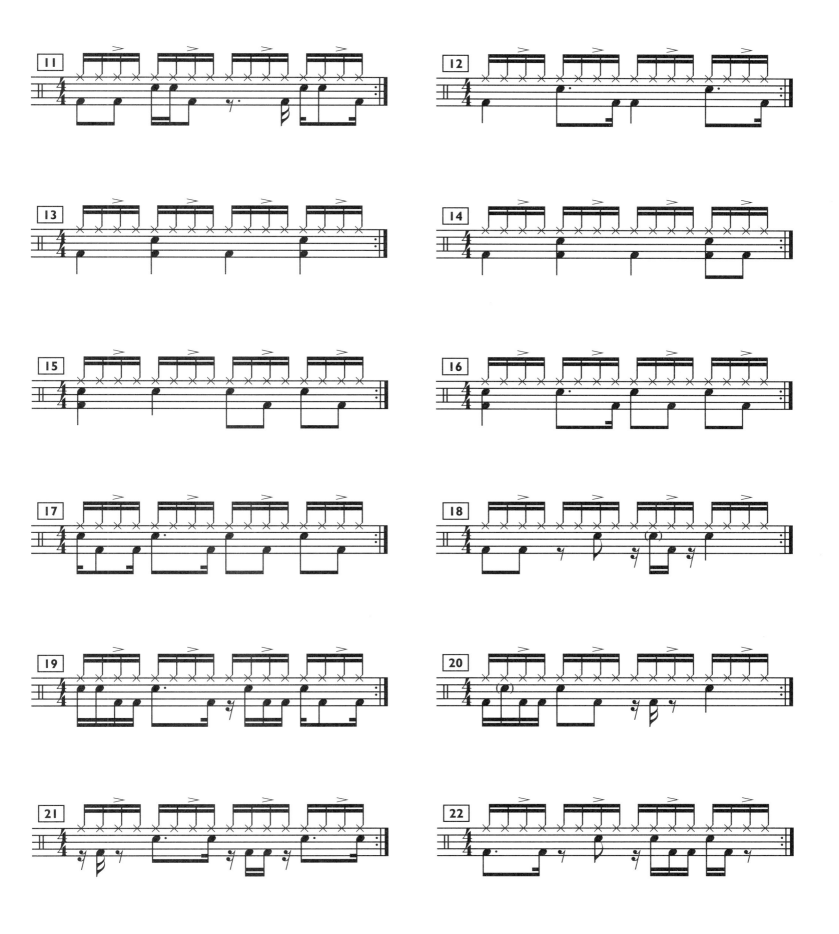

Part Twelve—Sixteenths with Snare on 2 and 4

In Part Twelve, the consistent sixteenth-note rhythm combined with the RLRL sticking causes us to leave out some hi-hat notes in order to hit the snare, as in examples such as 5 and 8. The important thing is to keep the sticking alternations and sixteenth-note subdivisions going at all times.

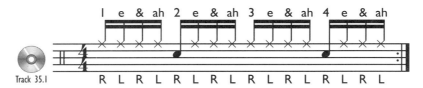

Track 35.1

Track 35.2

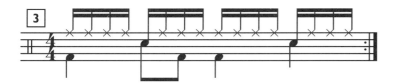

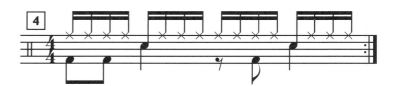

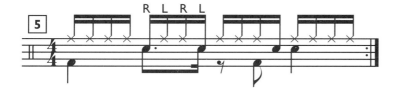

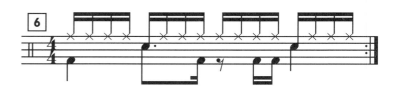

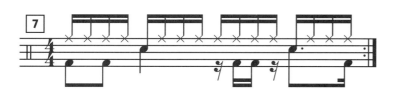

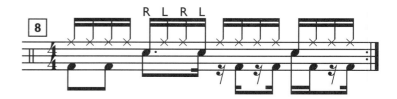

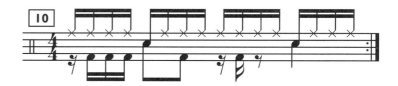

Part Thirteen—Sixteenths with Snare on 2 and 4 and Accents on the Offbeats

As in Part Twelve, the consistent sixteenth-note rhythm combined with the RLRL sticking in Part Thirteen causes us to leave out some hi-hat notes in order to hit the snare.

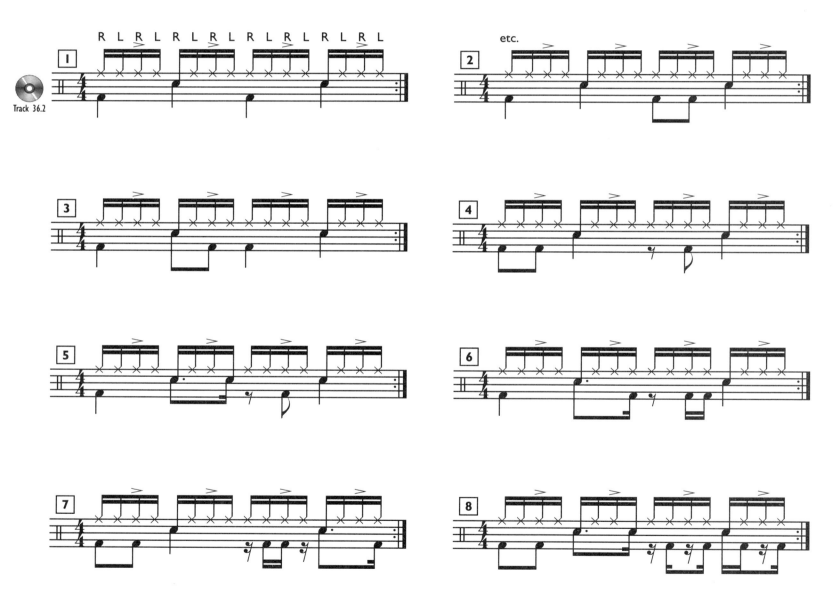

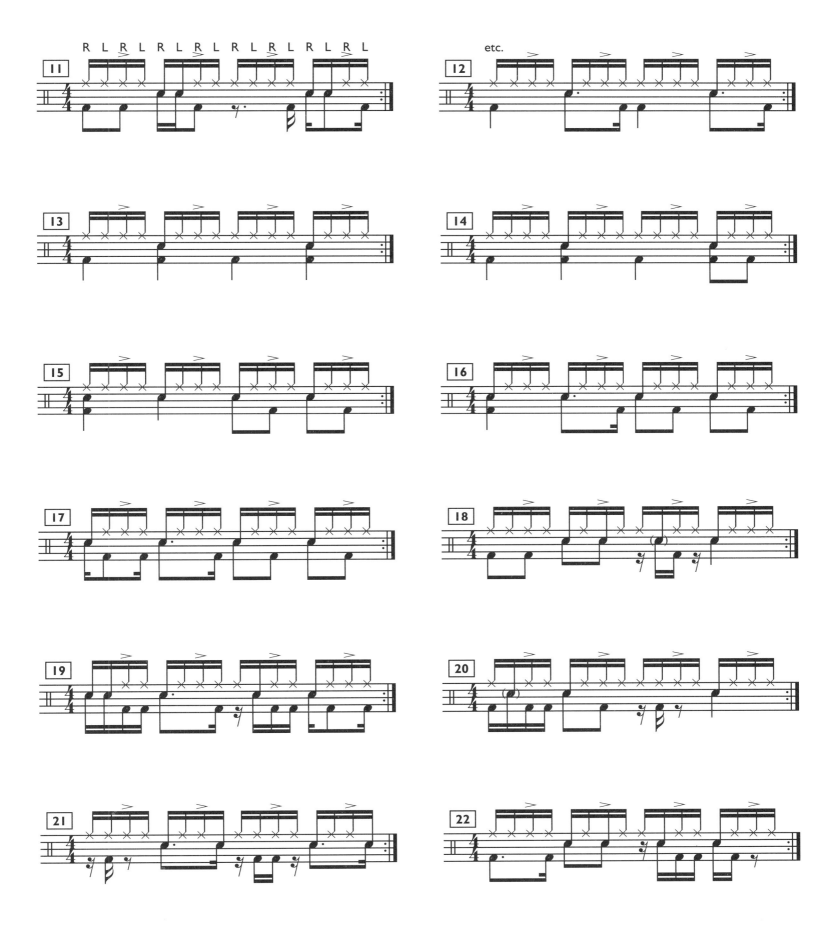

Part Fourteen—Sixteenths with Rests on the Onbeats

(1) e & ah (2) e & ah (3) e & ah (4) e & ah

Track 37.1

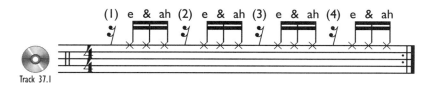

Track 37.2

1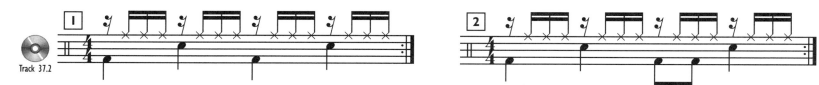

2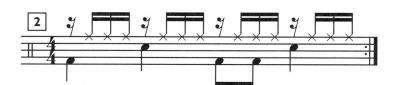

3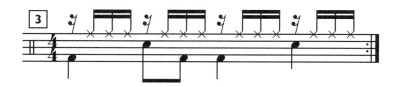

4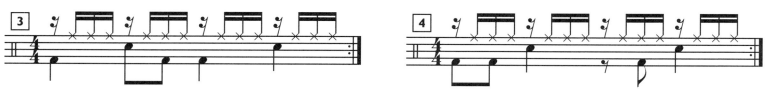

5

6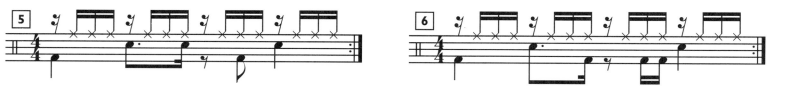

7

8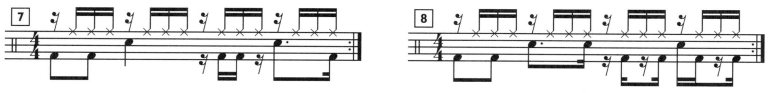

9

10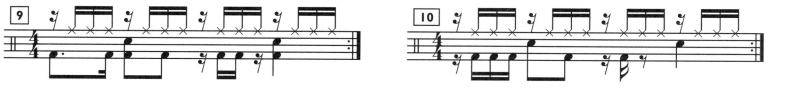

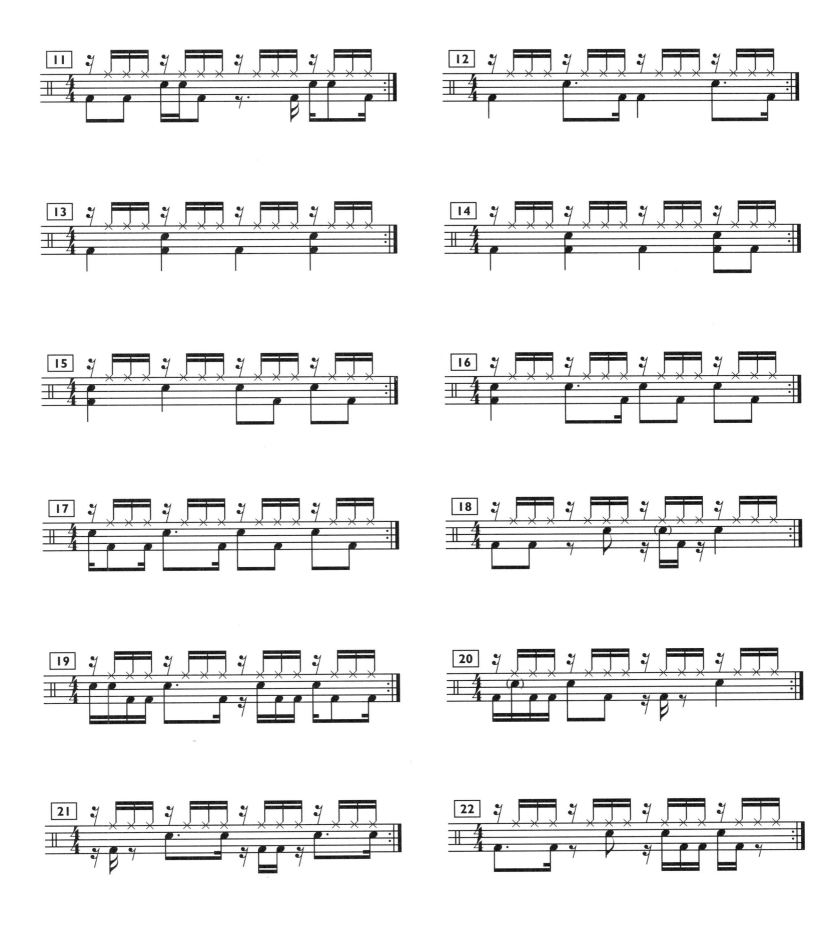

Part Fifteen—Sixteenths with Rests on the Onbeats and Accents on the Offbeats

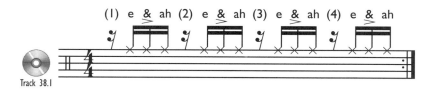

Track 38.1

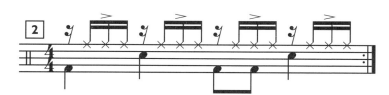

Track 38.2

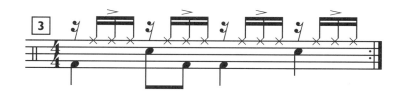

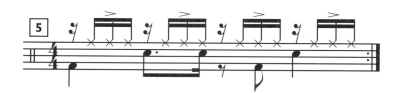
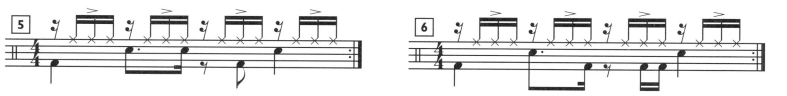

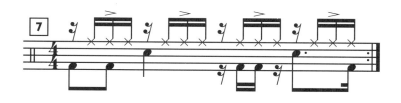
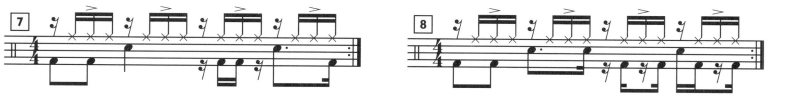

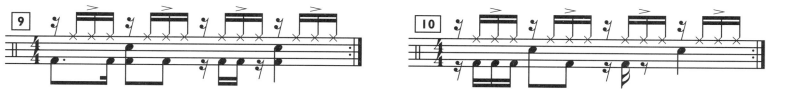

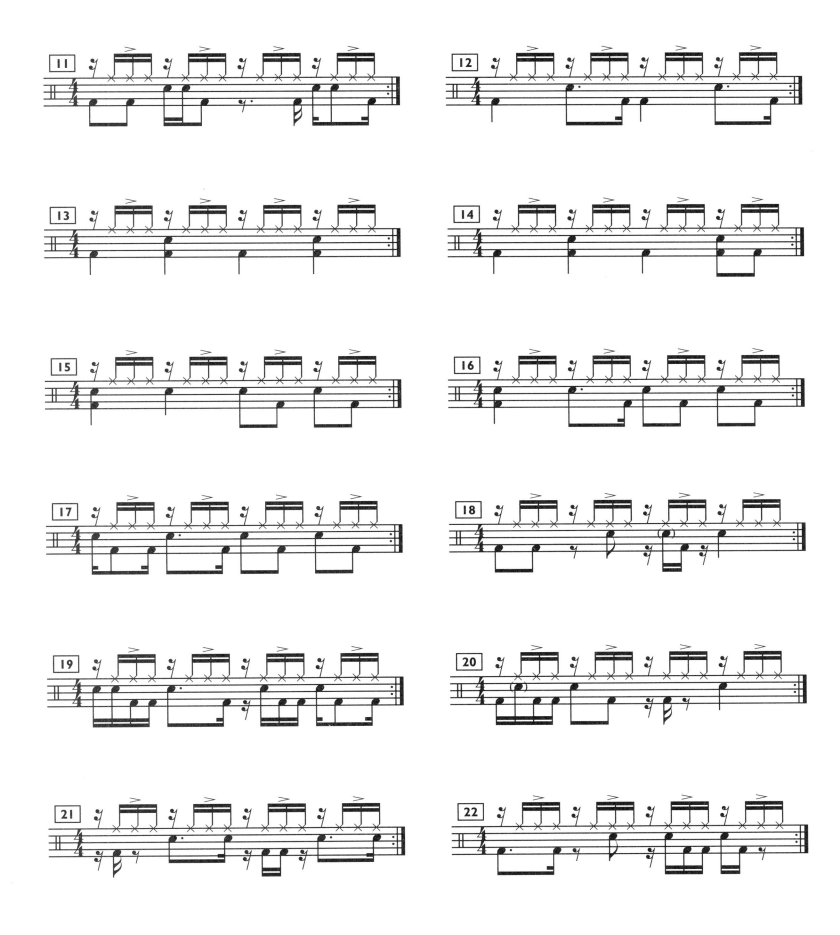

Part Sixteen—One Eighth and Two Sixteenths

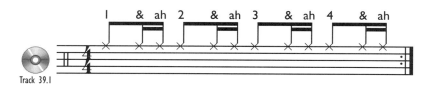

Track 39.1

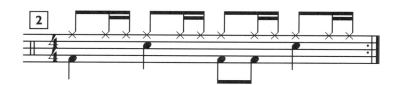

Track 39.2

| 1 | 2 |

| 3 | 4 |
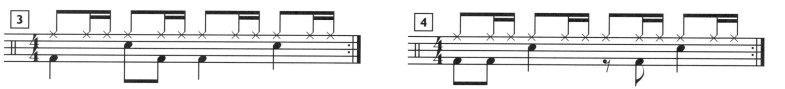

| 5 | 6 |
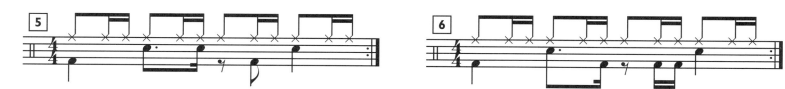

| 7 | 8 |
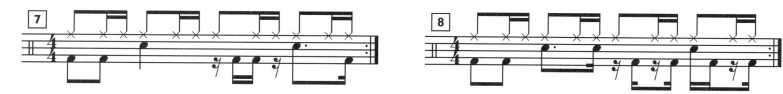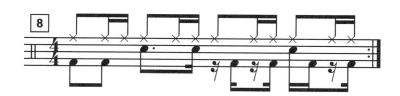

| 9 | 10 |
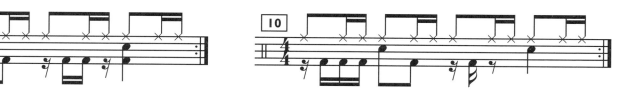

Part Seventeen—One Eighth and Two Sixteenths with Accents on the Onbeats

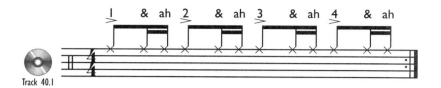

Part Eighteen—One Eighth and Two Sixteenths with Accents on the Offbeats

49

Part Nineteen—
Sixteenth/Eighth/Sixteenth

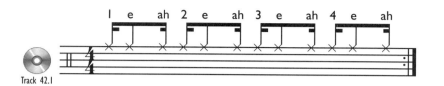

Track 42.1

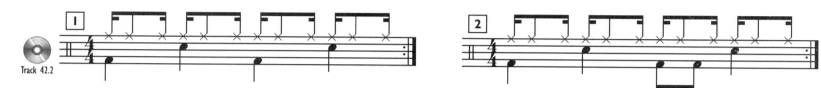

Track 42.2

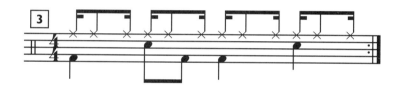

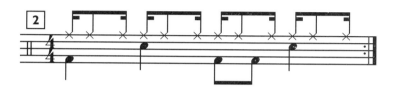

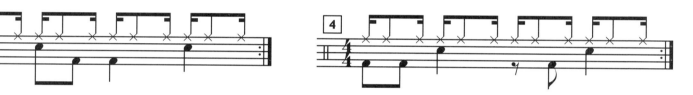

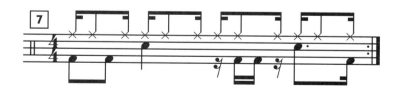

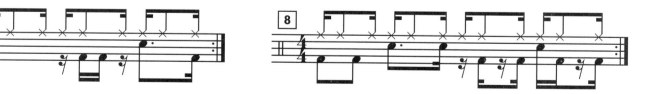

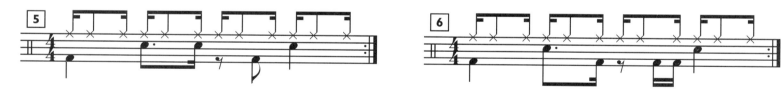

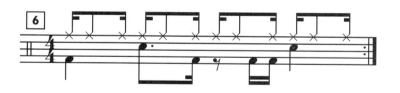

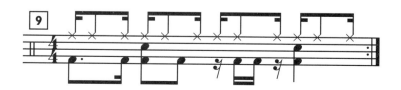

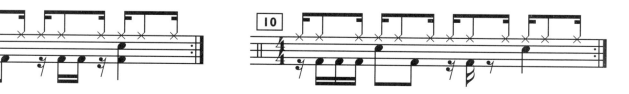

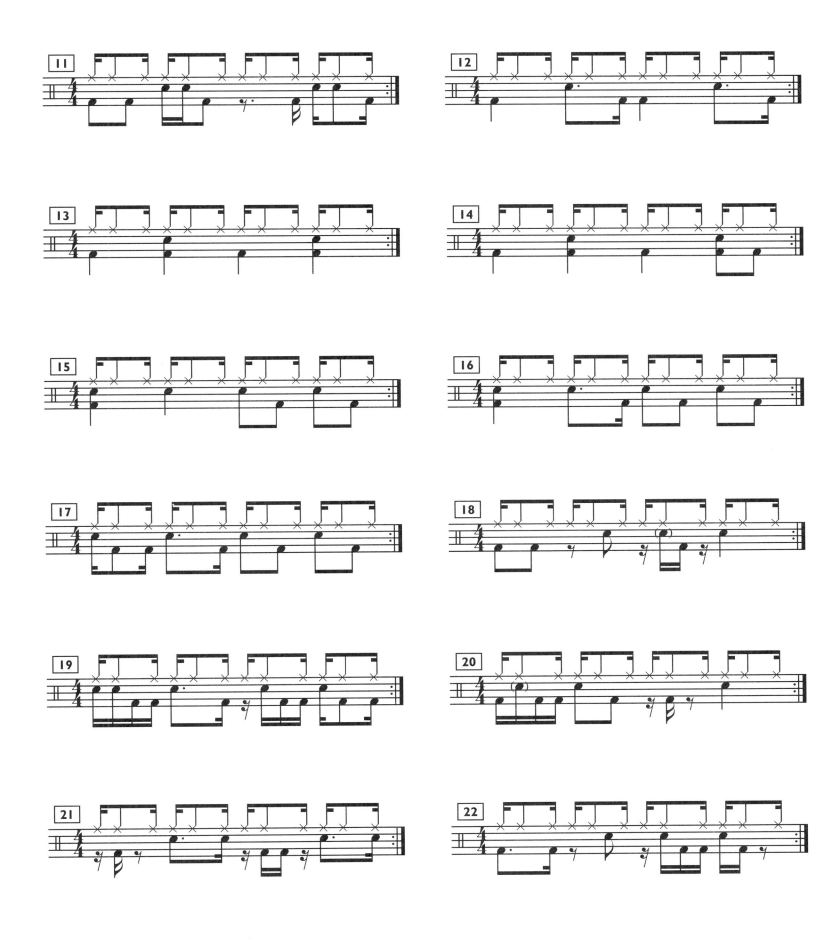

Part Twenty—Sixteenth/EIghth/Sixteenth with Accents on the Onbeats

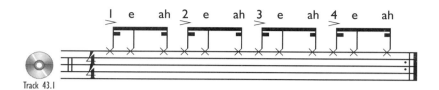

Track 43.1

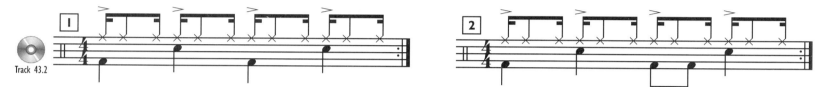

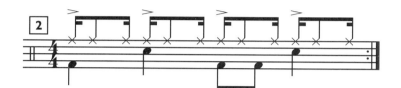

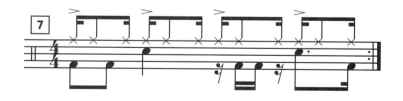

Track 43.2

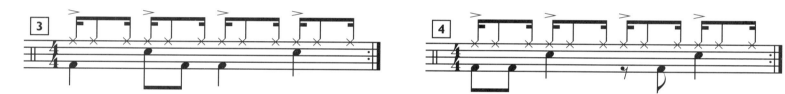

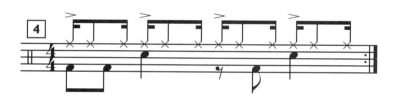

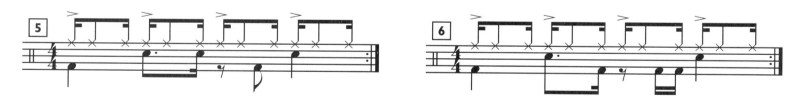

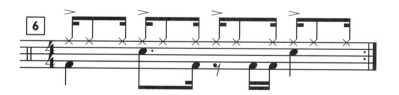

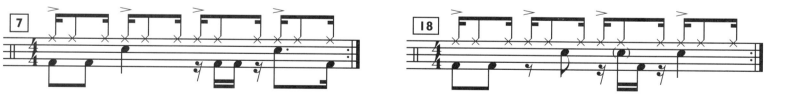

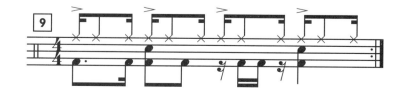

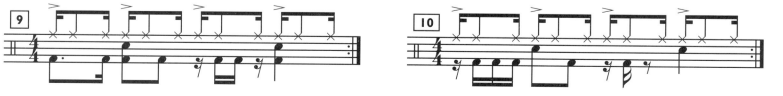

Part Twenty-One—Two Sixteenths and an Eighth

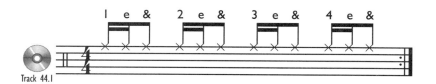

Track 44.1

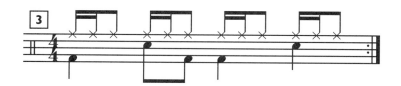

Track 44.2

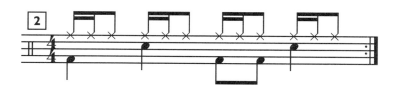

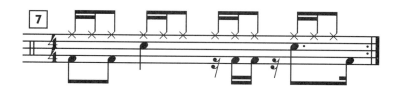

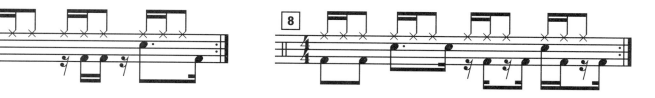

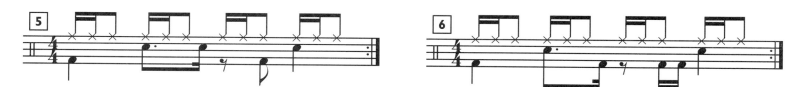

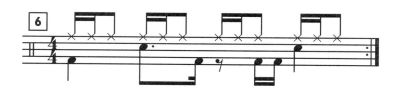

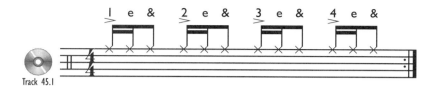

Part Twenty-Two—Two Sixteenths and an Eighth with Accents on the Onbeats

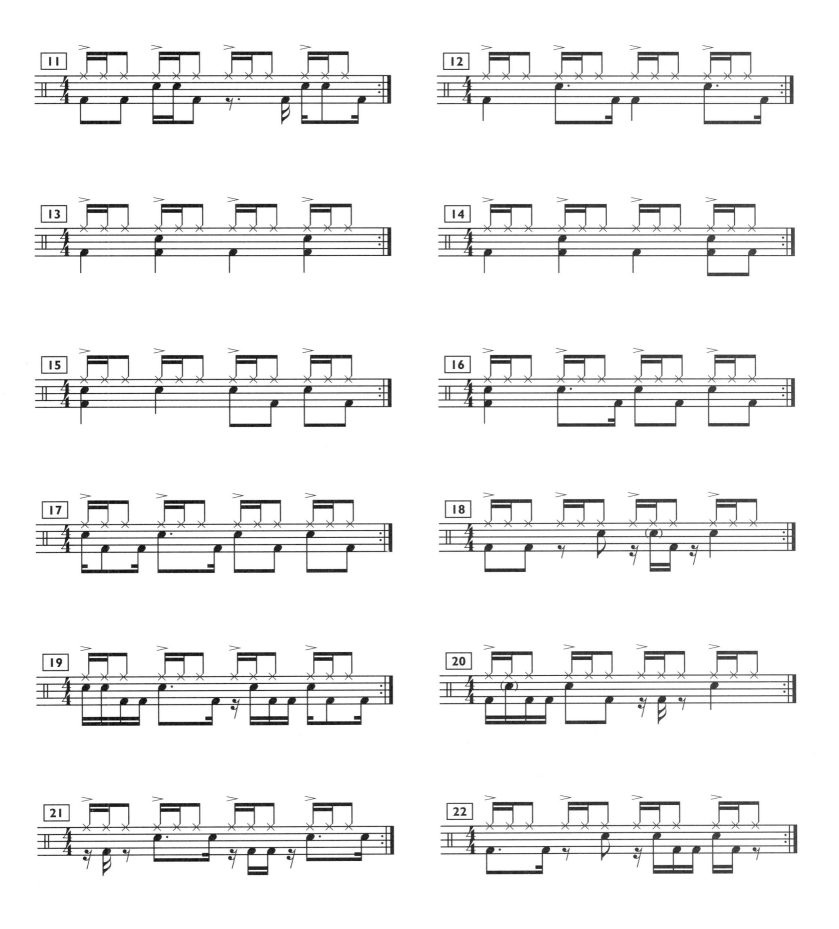

Part Twenty-Three—Two Sixteenths and an Eighth with Accents on the Offbeats

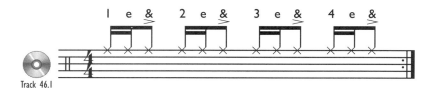

Track 46.1

Track 46.2

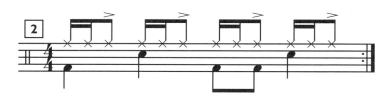

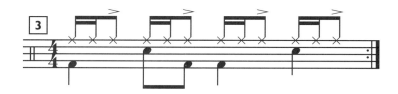

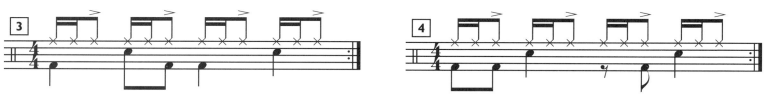

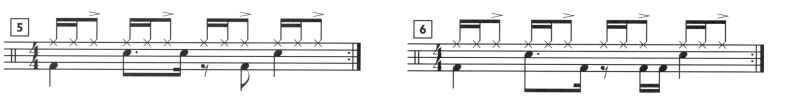

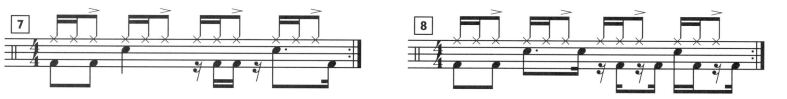

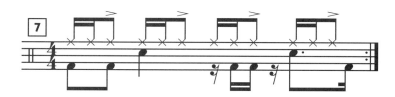

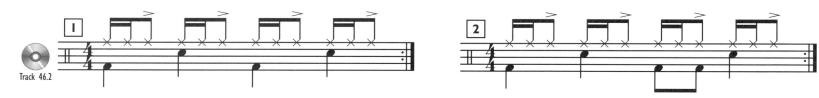

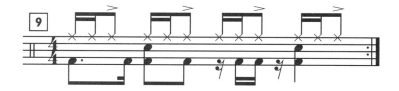

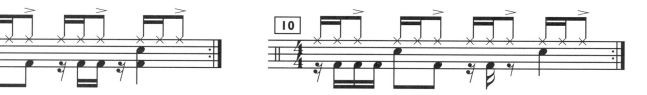

Part Twenty-Four—Dotted Eighth/Sixteenth

When playing rhythms that include dotted-eighth/sixteenth-note rhythms, be sure to carefully subdivide as you count (think sixteenths). This will help prevent the rhythms from sounding like quarter/eighth triplets.

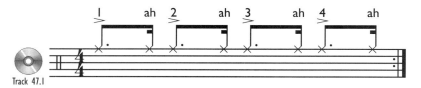

Track 47.1

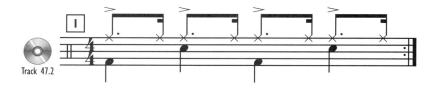
Track 47.2

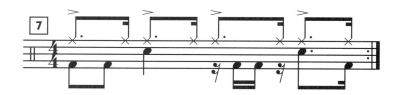

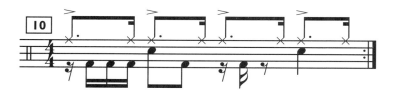

Part Twenty-Five—Two Sixteenths and an Eighth Rest

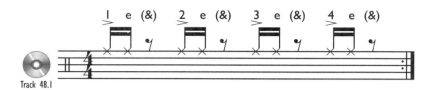

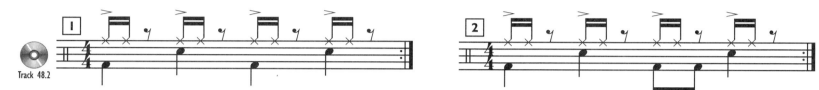

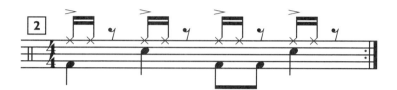

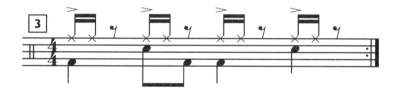

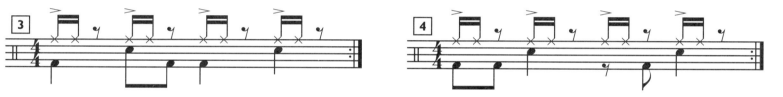

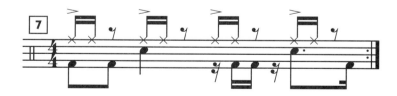

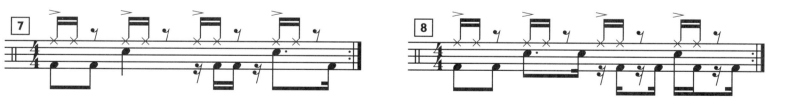

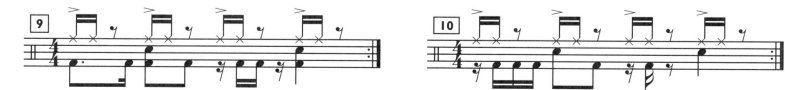

Track 48.1

Track 48.2

Part Twenty-Six—Sixteenth Rest and a Pair of Sixteenths

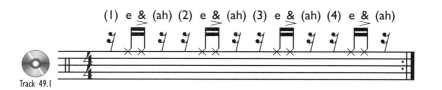

Track 49.1

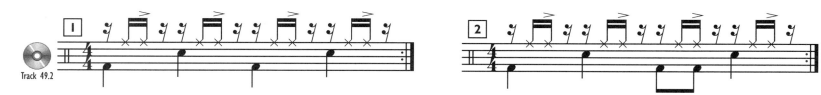

Track 49.2

1

2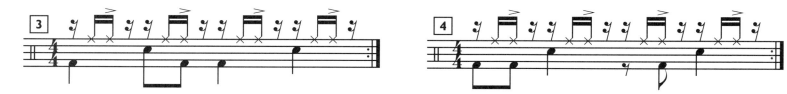

3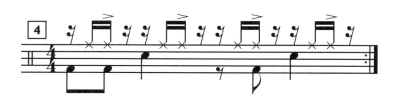

4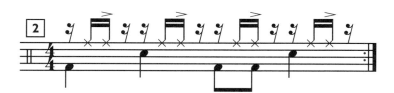

5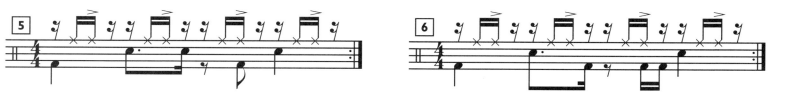

6

7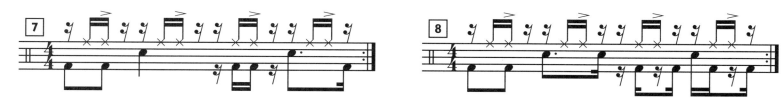

8

9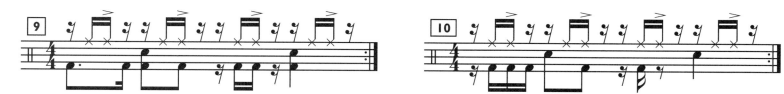

10

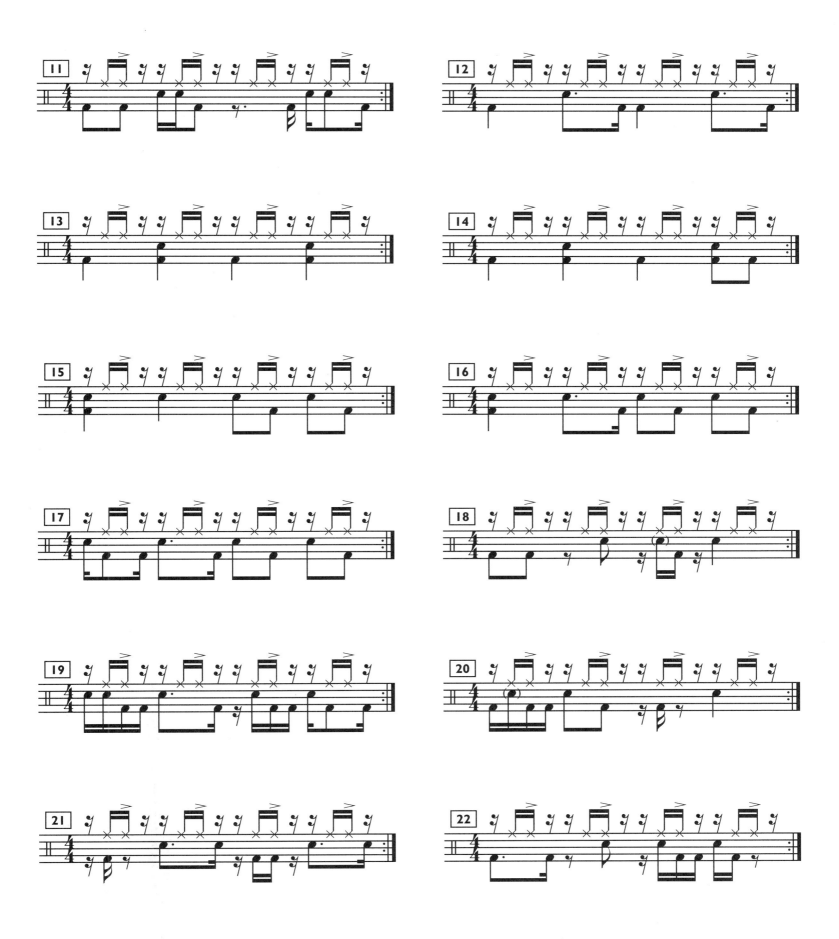

Part Twenty-Seven—Eighth Rest and a Pair of Sixteenths

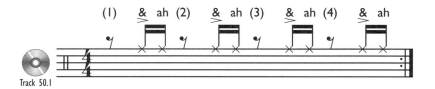

Track 50.1

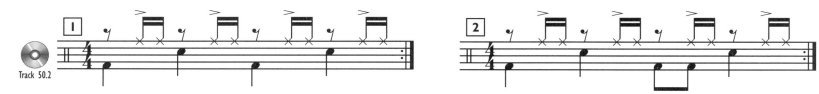

Track 50.2

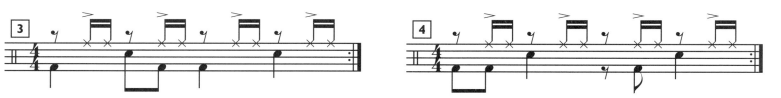

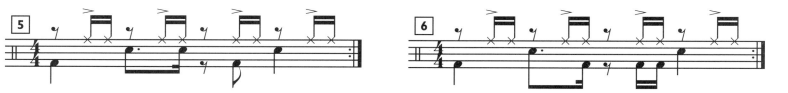

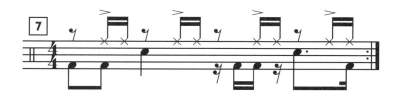

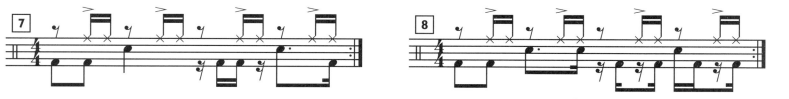

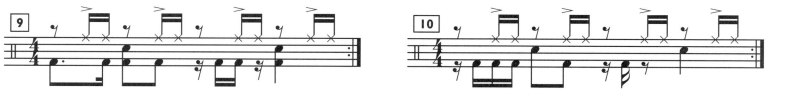

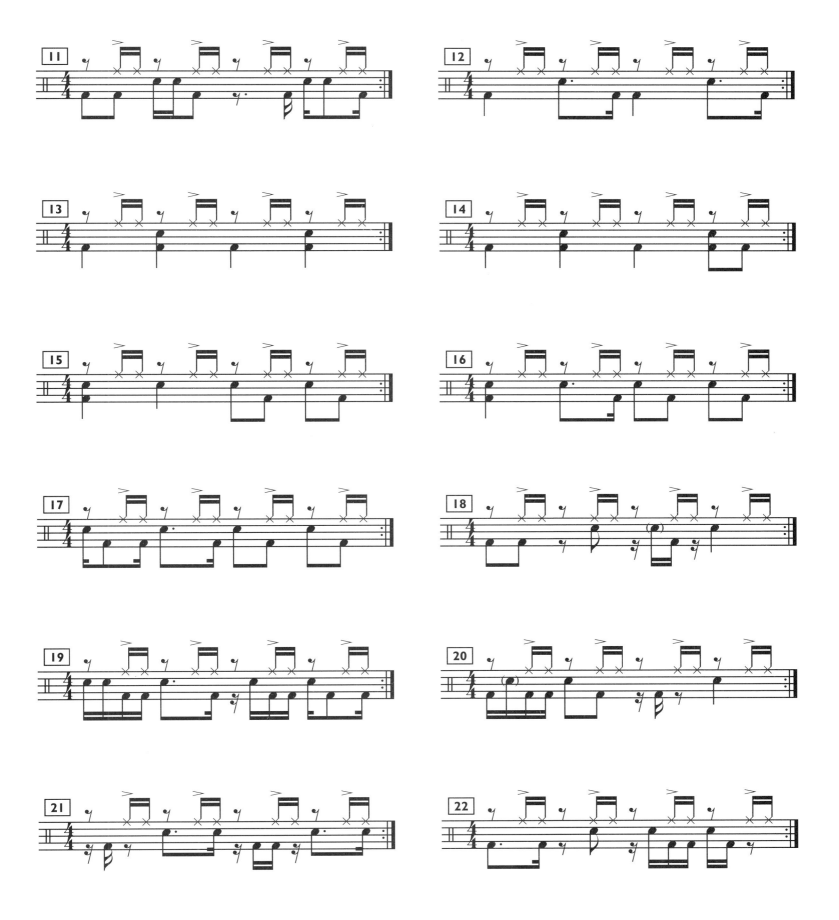

Part Twenty-Eight—Syncopated Sixteenths

(1) e (&) ah (2) e (&) ah (3) e (&) ah (4) e (&) ah

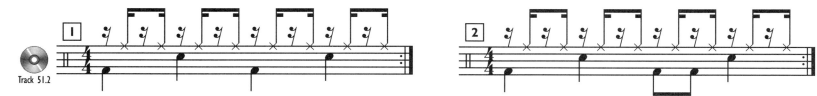

Track 51.1

Track 51.2

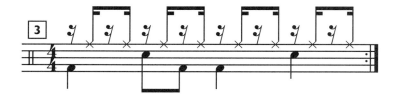

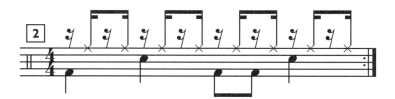

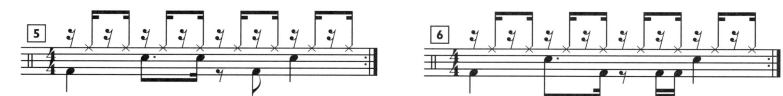

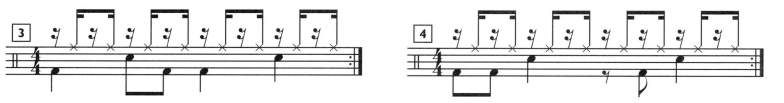

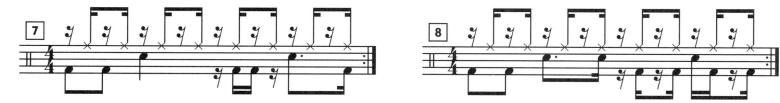

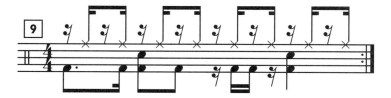

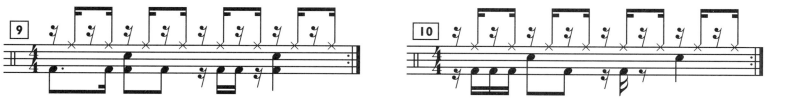

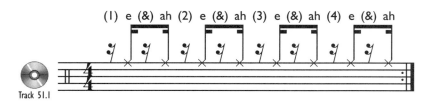

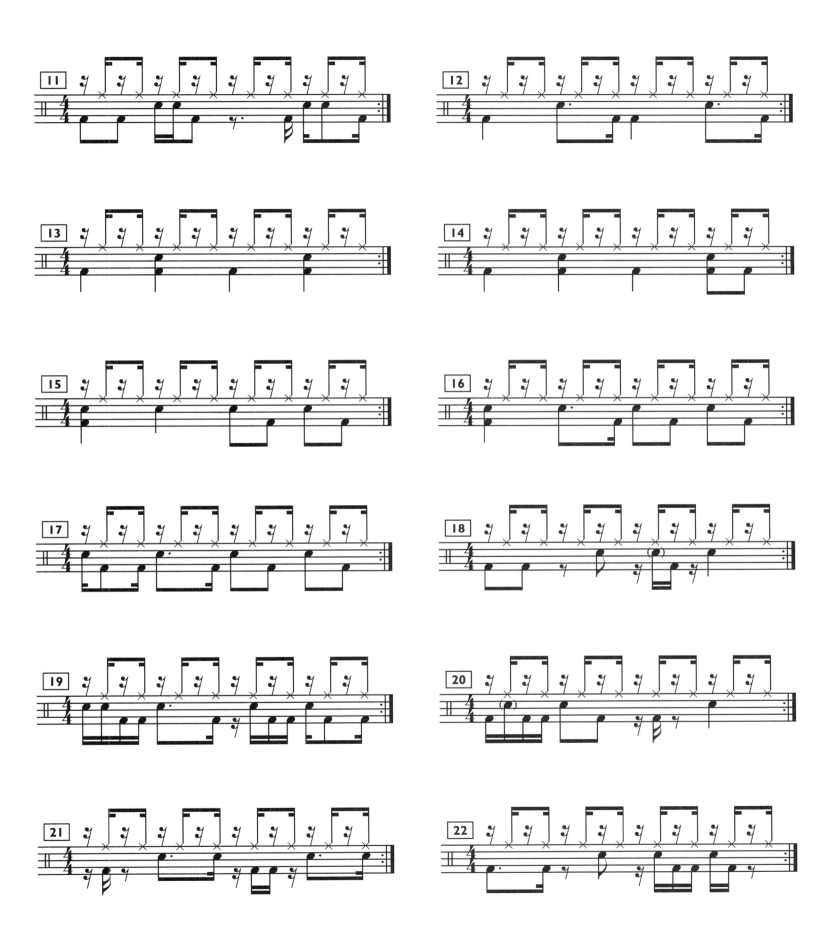

Section Two

Open Hi-Hat Development

"Let me simply restate what's been said by so many hundreds of times in this magazine: The fastest chops, the most blazing solos and funkiest fills in the world will never compensate for a drummer who cannot play with a solid groove and good time."

Ronald Spagnardi—*Modern Drummer*, June 2000

All of the open hi-hat variations should be practiced using the 22 grooves in Section 1, Part Four.

Part One—Eighth-Note Open Hi-Hat Development with a Basic Groove

For ease of learning, all 10 exercises below feature the same basic groove. The only change from one exercise to the next is the placement of the open hi-hat (o). The same exercise is repeated in Part Two of this section, with a more involved groove.

o = Open hi-hat.
+ = Closed hi-hat.

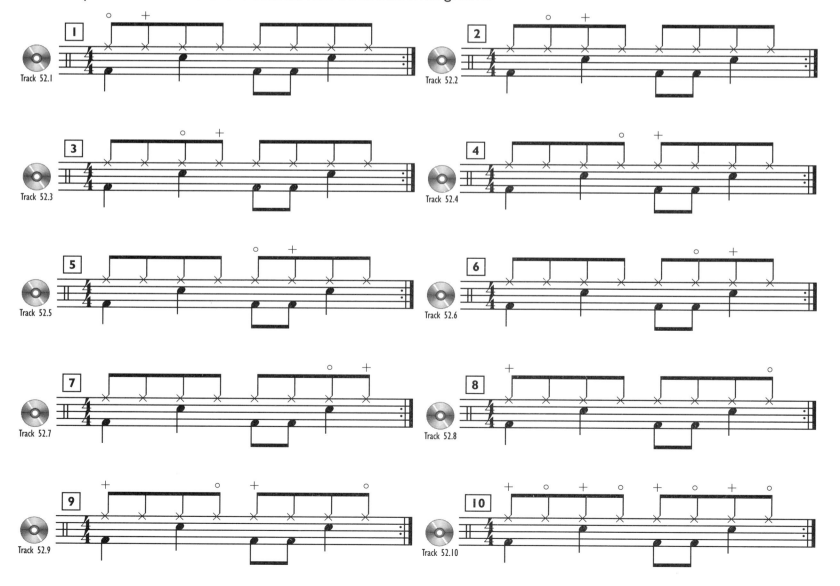

Part Two—Eighth-Note Open Hi-Hat Development with a More Involved Groove

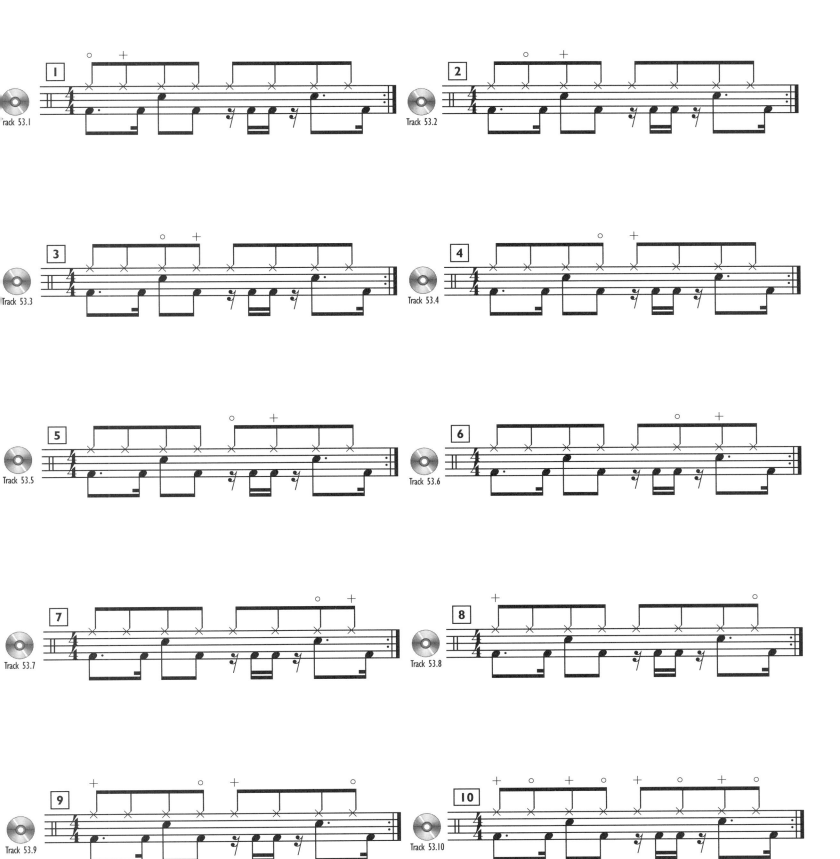

Part Three—Sixteenth-Note Open Hi-Hat Development Exercises With a Basic Groove

Part Four—Sixteenth-Note Open Hi-Hat Development Exercises with a More Involved Groove

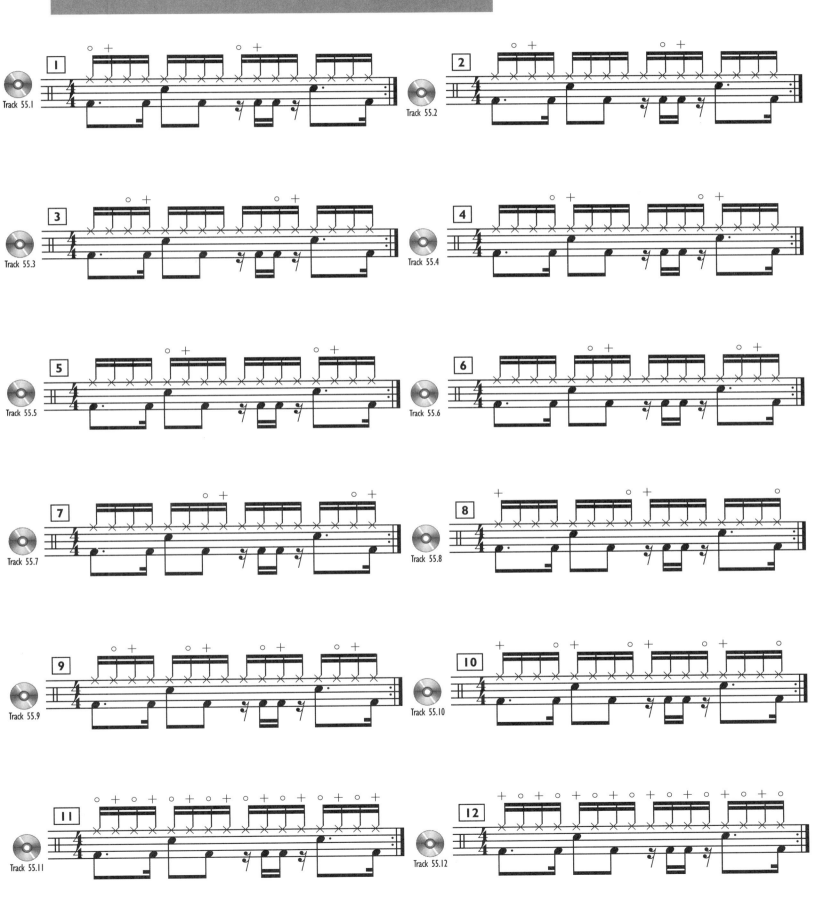

Part Five—Open Hi-Hat Development Exercises with a Basic Groove, Mixing Eighths and Sixteenths

You will notice that, from this page forward, the style of notation changes from two-voice, split stems to single-voice, linear notation (all stems up). This will make it clear how rhythms played on the kick and snare relate to the hi-hat. The exception to this is that some examples that have hi-hat played with the foot have the hi-hat stems down. Again, this is for clarity.

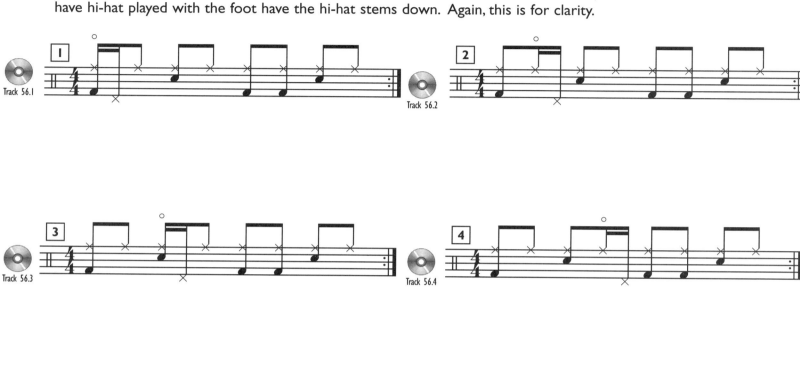

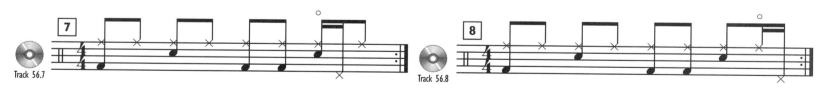

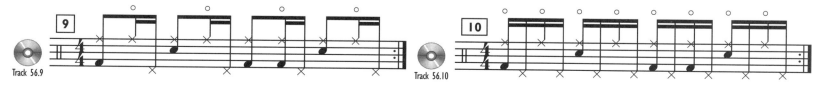

Part Six—Open Hi-Hat Development Exercises with a More Involved Groove, Mixing Eighths and Sixteenths

Part Seven—Summary of Section Two

Track 58.1

Track 58.2

Track 58.3

Track 58.4

Track 58.5

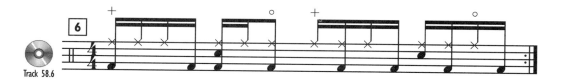

Track 58.6

Track 59.1

Track 59.2

Track 59.3

Track 59.4

Track 59.5

Track 59.6

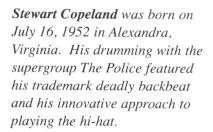

Stewart Copeland *was born on July 16, 1952 in Alexandra, Virginia. His drumming with the supergroup The Police featured his trademark deadly backbeat and his innovative approach to playing the hi-hat.*

*Session ace **Andy Newmark** was born on July 14, 1950, in Port Chester, New York. He is best known for his work on the Sly and the Family Stone 1973 release "Fresh."*

Section Three

Hi-Hat with the Foot

Clapping and *splashing* the hi-hat with the foot are highly effective techniques that may subtly—or drastically, depending on the execution—change the texture of any groove. These techniques are common in all time feels and are important elements of any drummer's training. Clapped notes produce a tight "chick" sound with the hi-hat cymbals and are played with a firm step at the top of your foot—near your toes. The splashed notes produce a loose "splash"-like sustain and are played with a heel kick at the bottom of the pedal with the bottom of your foot—the heel.

Clapping

Splashing

If you have the CD that is available for this book, listening to the examples in this section will be very helpful as you develop these techniques.

Below is a list of the contents of this section:

Page 80
Quarter Notes on the Hi-Hat with the Foot

*

Page 81
Quarter-Note Splashes on the Hi-Hat

*

Page 82
Eighth Notes on the Hi-Hat with the Foot

*

Page 83
Eighth-Note Splashes on the Hi-Hat with the Foot

*

Page 84
Playing the Hi-Hat on the Offbeats with the Foot

*

Page 85
Offbeat Splashes on the Hi-Hat

Part One—Quarter Notes on the Hi-Hat with the Foot

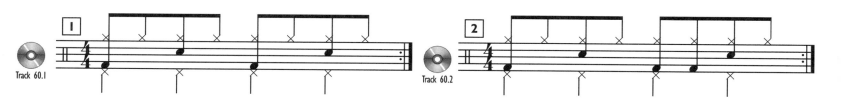

Track 60.1 · **1**

Track 60.2 · **2**

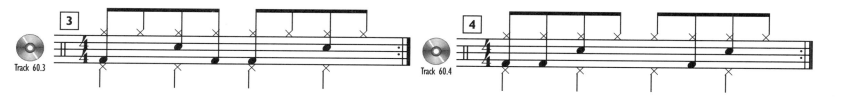

Track 60.3 · **3**

Track 60.4 · **4**

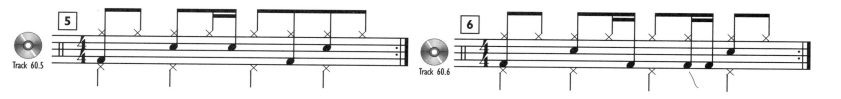

Track 60.5 · **5**

Track 60.6 · **6**

Track 60.7 · **7**

Track 60.8 · **8**

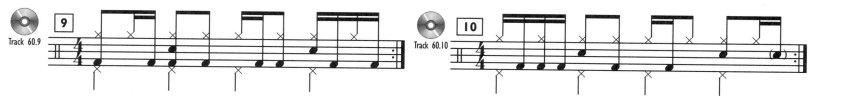

Track 60.9 · **9**

Track 60.10 · **10**

Part Two—Quarter-Note Splashes on the Hi-Hat

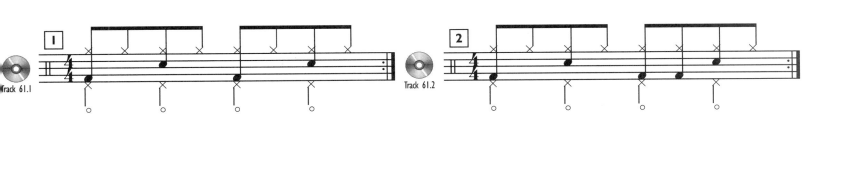

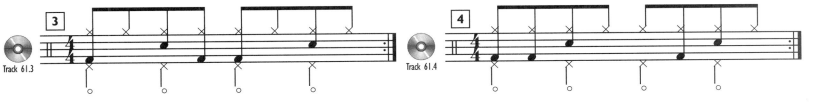

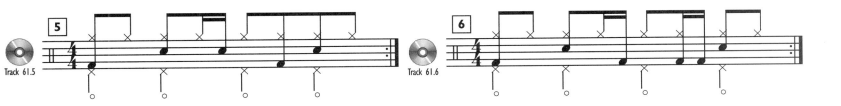

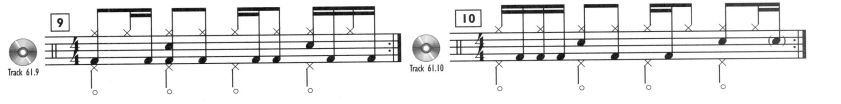

Part Three—Eighth Notes on the Hi-Hat with the Foot

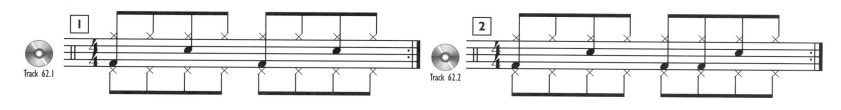

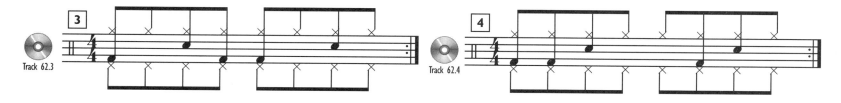

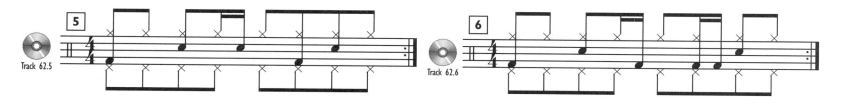

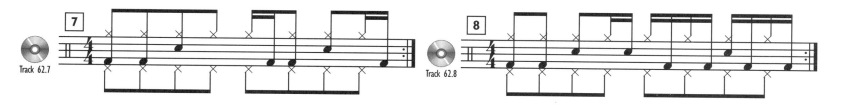

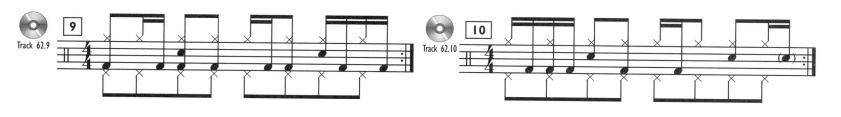

Part Four—Eighth-Note Splashes on the Hi-Hat with the Foot

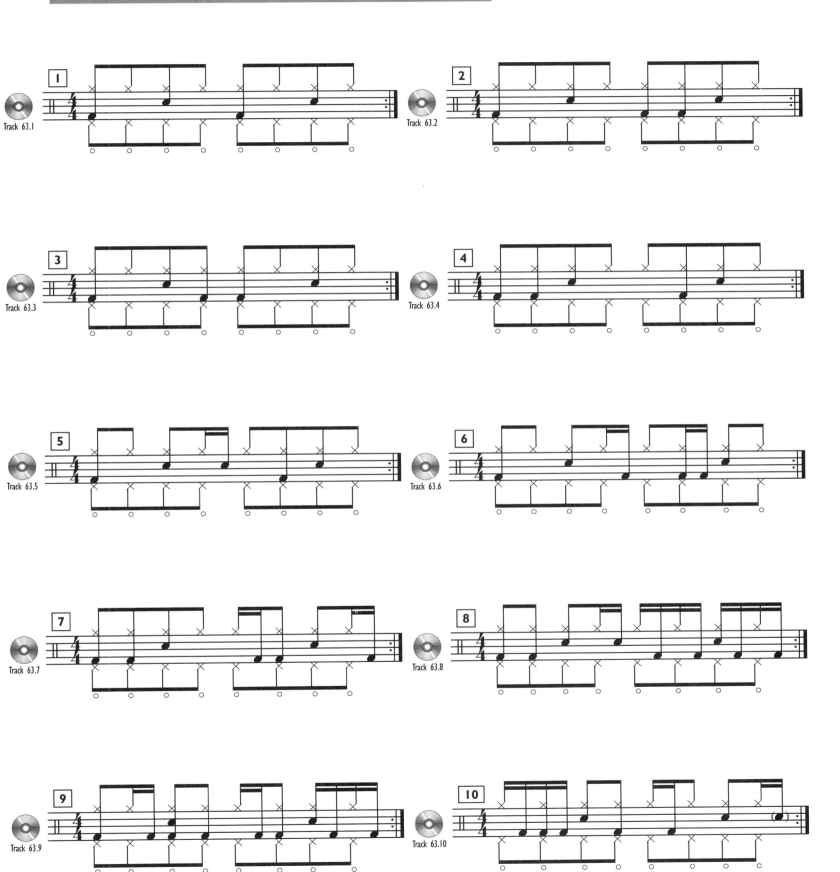

Track 63.1

Track 63.2

Track 63.3

Track 63.4

Track 63.5

Track 63.6

Track 63.7

Track 63.8

Track 63.9

Track 63.10

Part Five—Playing the Hi-Hat on the Offbeats with the Foot

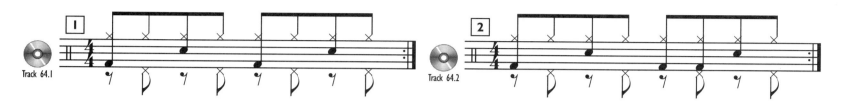

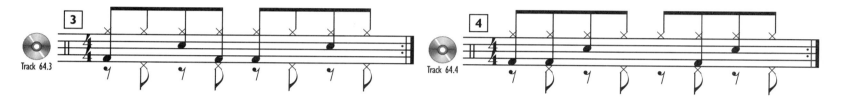

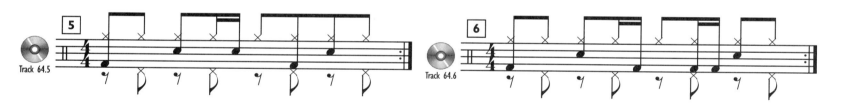

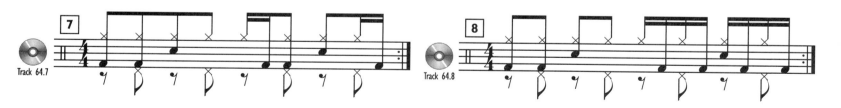

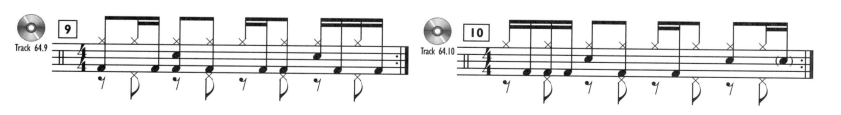

Part Six—Offbeat Splashes on the Hi-Hat

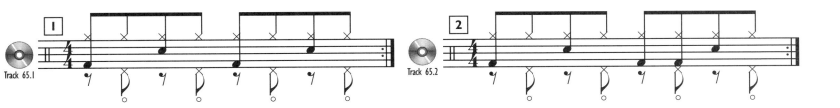

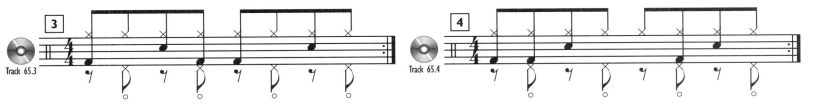

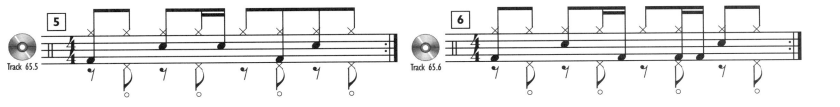

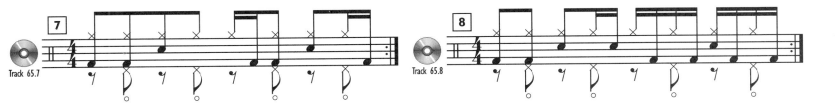

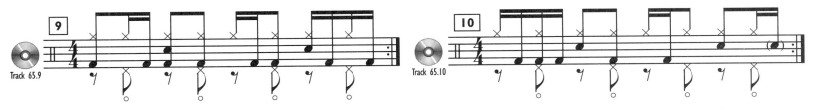

Section Four

Combining Clapped and Splashed Hi-Hat Notes with the Foot

The heel/toe foot technique is a commonly used method that allows you to easily and consistently execute clapped and splashed notes on the hi-hat. Although development of this technique is not necessary for performing these types of sounds, it is highly recommended.

The heel/toe technique is performed with the foot placed at the top of the hi-hat pedal. Since the clapped notes are played with the top of your foot and the splashed notes are played with with the bottom of your foot (see page 79), the heel/toe technique creates a rocking motion on the pedal.

The exercises in Part One of this section illustrate heel/toe technique using one basic groove. The focus is on the hi-hat. Part Two features a more involved groove using the same hi-hat exercises. Again, if you have the CD that is available for this book, you can use it as a reference.

Stevie Wonder was born on May 13, 1950, in Saginaw, Michigan. His approach to the drums is like his songwriting—heartfelt and honest. Listen to his playing on the tune Boogie On Reggae Woman *from his "Fulfillingness' First Finale" album and on the tune* Sugar *from his "Signed, Sealed and Delivered" album.*

Part One—A Basic Groove

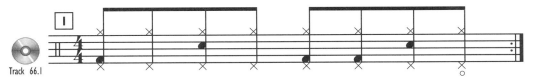

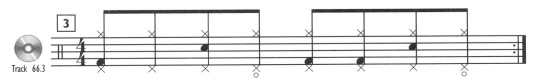

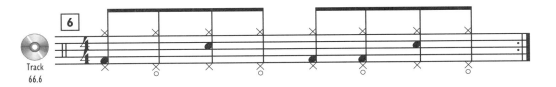

88

Part Two—A More Involved Groove

Track 67.1
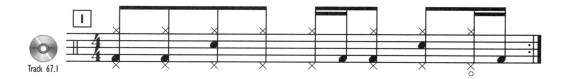

Track 67.2
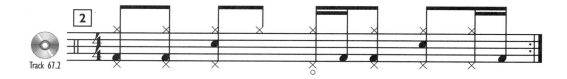

Track 67.3
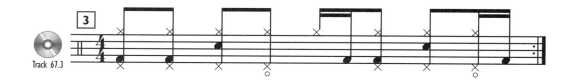

Track 67.4
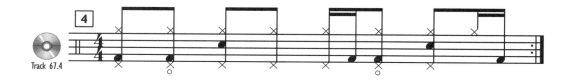

Track 67.5
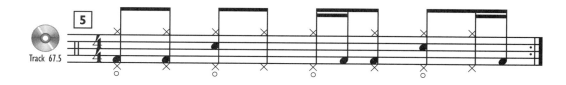

Track 67.6
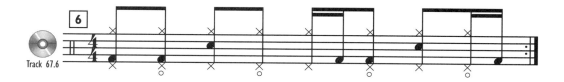

Section Five

Ghost Notes

Ghost notes are subtle, unaccented snare-drum notes that can be used to embellish any groove. These notes are played in addition to the main snare-drum notes that are part of the groove. Dynamically, ghost notes are executed at about half the volume of any backbeats or accented snare-drum notes.

The ghost notes in Part One of this section are written in parentheses. It may be helpful to first play each groove without the ghost notes. Once the main groove is established, add the ghost notes.

Part One of this section is a simple introduction to ghost notes using six different grooves. Part Two has the same six grooves, but they illustrate more involved ghost note interplay with the main notes. Some of these grooves are quite challenging but they are well worth the effort. If you have the CD that is available for this book, it will be a helpful reference for you.

PHOTO • CHUCK PULIN/COURTESY OF STAR FILE PHOTO, INC.

*Since the early 1970s, **Steve Jordan** has been on the "A" list of top session drummers. The classic recording by the Blues Brothers, "Briefcase Full of Blues" includes his most popular performances.*

Part One—Snare-Drum Ghost Notes with a Basic Groove

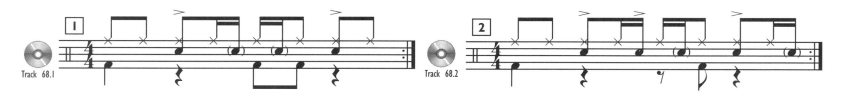

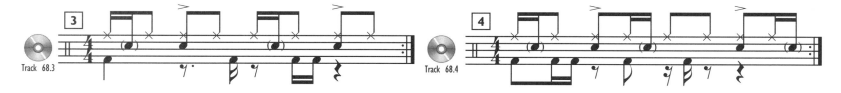

Part Two—More Involved Snare-Drum Ghost Notes

Section Six

New Grooves

This section provides some additional backbeat grooves for you to learn. Hopefully, they will stretch you a bit and excite your imagination. Try creating some of your own! Have fun!

"...focus on learning to play with a rhythm section. If you never lock in, you'll never get called."

Jabo Starks
Modern Drummer, September 1999

PHOTO • JEFF MAYER/COURTESY OF STAR FILE PHOTO, INC.

*Led Zeppelin drummer **John Bonham** (1948–1980) is the king of rock drumming. Checkout his relentless groove on the song* In the Evening *on the Led Zeppelin release,* "In Through the Out Door." *This is an overlooked Bonham groove gem.*

Track 70.1

Track 70.2

Track 70.3

Track 70.4

Track 70.5

Track 70.6

7 Track 71.1

8 Track 71.2

9 Track 71.3

10 Track 71.4

11 Track 71.5

12 Track 71.6

13 Track 72.1

14 Track 72.2

15 Track 72.3

16 Track 72.4

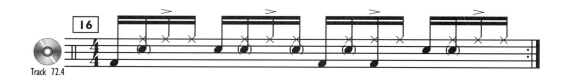

17 Track 72.5

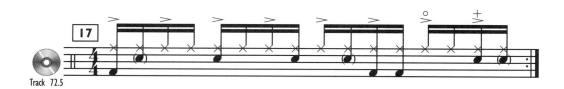

In Conclusion

I am pleased that you have chosen to make *The Drum Backbeat Encyclopedia* a part of your musical development, and I congratulate you in making the choice to expand you musical horizons. I am confident that working through this book has shaped and influenced your playing in a way that will prepare you to be a valuable asset in any group or playing situation the future may bring.

Because many of the techniques and examples illustrated in this book may take months or even years to master, I recommend regular use of the book as a reference guide for practicing. As time passes, and as you develop further as a groove player, you will find new meaning in many of the topics covered within these pages.

Developing great time and a great pocket is a gradual process. Reread the Introduction on page 4, the Muscle Memory section starting on page 7 and most importantly, follow the suggestions on how to listen in the Recommended Listening section on page 6. Immerse yourself in one recording at a time. What you listen to will have a far greater influence on your sound than any other musical training. You are what you listen to. In time, the influence of the music you surround yourself with will come out in your playing.

There is room in the world of music for everyone to participate. We all bring something unique and different to the table. If 50 drummers play the same groove on the same set of drums, they will all sound different. Who we are as people is reflected in the sound we produce on to our instruments. As we grow and mature through our lives, we grow and mature in our approach to music and to our instruments. Never let fear or insecurity stop you from being productive and working toward your goals. As we continue to practice, we also build confidence.

Use the following guidelines as the framework for developing your musicianship:

> 1) Play regularly with other musicians. Join or form a band.
> 2) Listen, listen, listen.
> 3) Practice and develop technique. Hone your skills. Take lessons.
> 4) Have fun!

Music is fun to learn and play. Maintaining a happy and healthy attitude is instrumental to your progress. Don't make music heavy. Approach it with a sense of humor. We all began to play because it is fun. As you realize the joyful experience of playing your instrument and playing with other musicians, learning and progress will happen naturally.

Remember, you can do anything you put your mind to. Persistence, patience and perseverance are all it takes. We are all blessed with the ability to learn and keep learning. The essence of the love that we experience through life and music is the journey. Spreading the love through music and enjoying the journey is the key.

I wish you success in all of your endeavors and look forward to hearing you groove.

You may contact John Thomakos at: www.johnthomakos.com